Veil

Veiling, Representation and Contemporary Art

Institute of International Visual Arts, London,
in association with Modern Art Oxford

Edited by David A. Bailey and Gilane Tawadros

Veil

Veiling, Representation and Contemporary Art

Published in the United Kingdom
by the Institute of International
Visual Arts (inIVA) in association
with Modern Art Oxford

Institute of
International Visual Arts
6–8 Standard Place
Rivington Street
London EC2A 3BE
www.iniva.org

© 2003 inIVA

Published on the occasion
of the exhibition *Veil*

The New Art Gallery Walsall, UK
14 February – 27 April 2003

Bluecoat Gallery and
Open Eye Gallery
Liverpool, UK
5 July – 16 August 2003

Modern Art Oxford, UK
22 November 2003 –
26 January 2004

Initiated by Zineb Sedira, developed
by Jananne Al-Ani and Sedira,
and curated by Al-Ani, David A.
Bailey, Sedira and Gilane Tawadros,
Veil is an inIVA touring exhibition.
The exhibition and accompanying
monograph are supported by the
Arts Council of England and the
Iran Heritage Foundation.

Texts © 2003, the authors
Images © 2003, the artists,
unless otherwise stated

ISBN 1-899846-35-2

A catalogue record of this book is
available from the British Library.

Designed by Untitled
Production co-ordinated
by Uwe Kraus
Printed in Italy

Front cover: Marc Garanger,
Femme Algérienne (Algerian
Woman), detail, 1960. Photograph,
30 x 40cm.
Back cover: Emily Jacir,
*From Paris to Riyadh (Drawings for
my Mother)*, detail, 1998–2001.
Marker on vellum, 24 x 28cm.

Notes on the
Transliteration of Arabic

Problems abound when attempting
to represent Arabic with the Roman
alphabet (transliteration) because
the sounds of Arabic and the rules
governing their combination
(phonology) differ greatly from
those of European languages. There
is no 'right way' to transliterate
Arabic, instead there are various
strategies tailored to the needs of
diverse readerships. Many writers
try to convey the sound of Arabic
words using the orthographic
conventions of their own language.
This can lead to a bewildering
multiplicity of forms. Even the
arbitrary systems devised to
represent Arabic phonology in
academic texts can differ in their
assignation of Roman letters,
symbols and diacritics. These
transliterations frequently incur
typesetting problems and can
appear overwrought and less than
illuminating to readers with no
Arabic. Some transliterated words
enter dictionaries in a standardised
form when repeated usage becomes
accepted usage (lexicalisation).

   Because this publication assumes
a readership unfamiliar with
Arabic, an arbitrary but consistent
system combining lexicalisation
and simplification is used for
transliterations. This means that
certain distinctions between Arabic
sounds are not represented, while
some sounds are omitted altogether.
However, this approach only
applies to the newly commissioned
articles; text reproduced from
previously published sources has
not been amended. Consequently,
unavoidable inconsistencies appear
between articles and even within
articles themselves.
Aidan Higgins

MODERN ART OXFORD

THE ARTS COUNCIL OF ENGLAND

LONDON ARTS

IRAN HERITAGE FOUNDATION

Why is it that this item of clothing has had such a huge impact on our culture? In a popular sense, the veil relates to a number of themes within our social climate, among them, questions of dress code, social status and the notion of the traditional. From a historical perspective, one can see these earlier obsessions with the veil in the discourse of travelogue writings over the last two hundred years; in postcard imagery; in Western literature; in nineteenth-century photography; in painting; and in early cinema. It is within these arenas of mass communication and popular culture that one can identify what Edward Said has described as the beginnings of Orientalism re-imagined within visual culture. In the context of the commodity branding of adornment within a globalised world and especially post-11 September, the veil has assumed new significance in the context of worldwide debates on multiculturalism. In contemporary Europe, more specifically, the veil is a persistent symbol of Europe's struggle to come to terms with cultural diversity and social inclusion.

It is important to discuss the process of how this project emerged and to give insight into the various collaborations which have taken place between a number of organisations and individuals. Initiated by Zineb Sedira, the exhibition was formally originated in 1998 by an application – made by Autograph: The Association of Black Photographers under the guidance and support of the Director Mark Sealy and David A. Bailey – to the Arts Council of England's Exhibition Research and Development Fund. This grant provided valuable support to Zineb Sedira and Jananne Al-Ani, enabling them to research, explore and develop this subject and to look for collaborators in the form of writers, artists and institutions. It was at this point that inIVA (Institute of International Visual Arts) came on board. The research and development phase led to a successful application to the Arts Council's National Touring Fund for the exhibition production and tour, a grant for which we are truly grateful. The final curatorial team responsible for the selection of artworks comprises Jananne Al-Ani, David A. Bailey, Zineb Sedira and Gilane Tawadros and the exhibition is produced with the support of the inIVA team, in particular Bruce Haines, assisted by Mahita El Bacha Urieta. Edited by Bailey and Tawadros, and compiled by Sarah Campbell, *Veil: Veiling, Representation and Contemporary Art* is published by inIVA in association with Modern Art Oxford.

The uniqueness of the curatorial narrative of the exhibition and its juxtaposition of commissioned works with existing pieces is discussed in depth in the introduction to this publication. Many of the works have been specially conceived for, or re-presented in, the spaces of each collaborating institution in a way that develops the exhibition's themes and issues with different emphases. We wish to thank the artists for agreeing to take part in what has been an ambitious venture. The variety of perspectives, genres and historical periods encompassed by the exhibition is embraced by this publication, in which newly commissioned contributions examine the theme of the veil alongside key historical texts that explore its presence within aspects of the visual arts, film and literature. We are grateful to Jananne Al-Ani, Alison Donnell, Reina Lewis, Hamid Naficy and Zineb Sedira for their thoughtful contributions.

We also extend our thanks to our institutional collaborators: the New Art Gallery Walsall; the Open Eye Gallery and the Bluecoat Gallery in Liverpool; and Modern Art Oxford. Not least, we are grateful to our lenders: the Arts Council Collection; the Collections of Eileen and Peter Norton, Santa Monica; the Musée de l'Homme; the British Film Institute; Fonds National d'Art Contemporain, Paris; and Fonds Régional d'Art Contemporain Provence-Alpes-Côtes d'Azur who have responded so generously and positively to our requests to borrow works.

Foreword
David A. Bailey
Suzanne Cotter, Modern Art Oxford
Gilane Tawadros, inIVA

Exhibiting Artists

Faisal Abdu'Allah
Kourush Adim
AES art group
Jananne Al-Ani
Ghada Amer
Farah Bajull
Samta Benyahia
Gaëtan de Clérambault
Marc Garanger
Shadafarin Ghadirian
Ghazel
Emily Jacir
Ramesh Kalkur
Majida Khattari
Shirin Neshat
Harold Offeh
Gillo Pontecorvo
Zineb Sedira
Elin Strand
Mitra Tabrizian

Preface
Reina Lewis

The veil is an item of clothing dramatically overburdened with competing symbolism. This publication and the exhibition it accompanies offer a welcome chance to address the gap between individual experiences of veiling and its complex and contested status in a variety of public arenas. In an agenda-setting selection, this project unites historical material, personal accounts and critical writing with contemporary visual art to show how the heterogeneous use of veiling, as dress act and visual trope, is endlessly repositioned by changing world events and constantly reframed by the nuanced shifting responses of veiling communities.

For women who wear it and artists who represent it, the veil is a garment whose meaning cannot be contained. It is a garment fought over by adherents and opponents, many of whom claim that their understanding of the veil's significance is the one and true meaning. But as this project demonstrates, if the secret imagined to lie behind the veil reveals one thing, it is that it cannot be contained within a single truth, experience or understanding. Instead, the veil emerges as a form of clothing that is rooted in specific historical moments and locations; its depiction is similarly contingent and its adoption, adaptation and rejection is always itself relational.

For the West, long obsessed with seeing behind the veil, the veil stands for the fantasised absolute divide behind East and West. Within a binarised worldview, penetrating behind the veil is the key to the mysteries of the East and a route to the penetration of territory (symbolic and literal). Seen often as proof of the oppression of Muslim women or as a marker of cultural difference in need of 'toleration', the veil has always and continues to excite strong reactions and counter-reactions. For women who wear the veil, or who come from veil-wearing societies even if they themselves do not veil, Western attitudes (and their local take-up) cannot be avoided. But wearing a veil is a dress act whose level of volition or compunction varies for each community and for each woman. Moreover, in the space of a single woman's lifetime, the reasons that affect her decision to cover herself and the ways in which this is achieved can vary in response to personal, geographical, social and political events. Negotiating with local, national or diasporic community gender systems is never an isolated event when the figure of the veiled woman is fought over as emblematic of whole societies.

Today the veil is almost always regarded as an Islamic institution and is often claimed as such. Though it is now predominantly associated with Muslims and Islam, in the past veiling was a social practice shared by many populations in the Middle East and North Africa, where to veil spoke of status rather than religion. Like the harem system's division of space, the veil was part of a system of gender seclusion that impacted more on the rich than the poor, more on the urban than the rural and that co-opted men into reciprocally modest behaviours. But these practices never occurred in isolation and changes in veiling habits came about and come about not only in relation to local developments but also through interaction with the West. The emergence of local forms of modernity and postmodernity marked by the engagement (forced and voluntary) with Western ideologies, markets and cultural forms, produces shifts in the perceived local and international significance of the veil. Standing as a beacon of tradition or an emblem of progressive modernity, the veiled or unveiled, de-veiled or re-veiled woman has been a feature of divergent struggles over decolonisation, nationalism, revolution, Westernisation and anti-Westernisation.

In all of these developments women's agency has been central as they struggle to deal with the myriad ways in which the figure of woman becomes symbolic for all sides of political debate. Yet the veil is often read by the West as evidence of the very denial of women's

Preface
Reina Lewis

Shirin Neshat, *Rapture*, 1999.
Film still, 13 mins. Collections
of Eileen and Peter Norton,
Santa Monica.

AES art group, *New Freedom 2006, AES – The Witnesses of the Future*, 1996. Photographs.

agency, or is over-inflated into the most important feminist struggle. But, in fact, for many women the requirement to veil is often the least of their problems in the face of economic and social deprivation. In other instances, women's veiling is strategic, providing an alibi for behaviours outside the home that would otherwise be deemed gender subversive. Though the potential liberation afforded by veiling is recognised by some earlier Western travellers, the myth that seclusion equals subordination continues to structure attitudes to veiling in the West and among those postcolonial regimes characterised by aggressive secularisation. Thus women, in their public presentation, navigate a complex dialectic of local patriarchies and international politics.

These loaded social and (sometimes) personal conditions are also the context within which artists make representations of the veil. In addition, their work and its reception is bound to be positioned in relation to existing visual conventions in the depiction of the veil. From Western Orientalist painting to movies to media current affairs, coverage of the veiled woman continues to haunt the visual imagination, reincarnated in contemporary terms that inevitably owe an allegiance to longstanding misapprehensions about the nature of veiled life. Rather than simply offering a corrective to this well-established visual iconography, *Veil: Veiling, Representation and Contemporary Art* selects work that not only shows the variety of visual response to veiling, but that also foregrounds the contingency of the viewer's interpretation. The different experiences and cultural and historical knowledges that viewers bring to the artworks discussed here and seen in the exhibition mean that a number of readings can emerge. This accommodation of differently constructed interpretive communities challenges the closing down of meaning that artists from veiling backgrounds often experience, since diasporic artists, particularly those who feature the veil in their work, frequently find that they are categorised regionally or exclusively in relation to Islam.

It thus remains a matter of political and cultural urgency to reconceptualise the economy of multiple gazes that filter through, slide off and remake the veil. This project is one such opportunity.

Mohsen Makhmalbaf, *Kandahar*, 2001. Film still. © WildBunch. Under the cover of a burka, Nafas, the protagonist of *Kandahar*, disguises herself as an Afghan wife in order to attempt her journey back to the Taliban-controlled city of Kandahar.

Samta Benyahia, *Femme
Haracta des Aurès* (Woman
from Harachta des Aurès), 1997.
Photograph, 116 x 95cm.

Introduction
David A. Bailey and Gilane Tawadros

Veil. The word alone conjures up images in the mind's eye. In the aftermath of 11 September, the veil has become synonymous with cultural and religious differences that have been presented to us repeatedly as unbridgeable, alien and terrifying. The fact that the veil and veiling have been a part of both Western and Eastern cultures for millennia, from the aristocratic women of ancient Greece to contemporary brides worldwide, has not diminished from their overwhelming association with Islam and an abstract, exoticised notion of the East.[1]

This project was conceived long before the events of 11 September. The concept of Zineb Sedira, it was researched and developed by Sedira and Jananne Al-Ani over a period of four years and emerges directly from their practice as visual artists. For Al-Ani and Sedira, the significance of the veil lies in its complex and multiple meanings. As Al-Ani points out in her essay, the work of artists in this exhibition re-presents the veil from plural and complex viewpoints and against the grain of written histories: '[The works] have been generated, often with wonderful humour, by artists with an intimate knowledge of both Western and Eastern cultures.... Through their work, the artists have helped to broaden the debate on representation and the veil in a complex and provocative way and to sow doubts about the facts of the past, by looking at something we think we know and understand.'[2]

For Sedira, the veil is not simply a physical code or visual motif but rather elicits 'a multitude of readings, both visible and invisible'. As she writes of her practice as an artist: 'Veiling-the-mind has become a metaphor of mine for the (mis)reading of cultural signs... in order to explore the multiple forms of veiling in both Western and Muslim cultures. I find myself asking how to "represent the unrepresentable" and my artistic interventions reveal my desire to open up the paradoxes, ambiguities and symbolism of the veil.'[3] In her essay entitled 'The Language of the Veil',

Ahdaf Soueif points out that there is no single word in Arabic equivalent to 'the veil'; while its physical manifestations are as varied as the social, historical and cultural contexts in which it is to be found: 'To the west, "the veil" like Islam itself, is both sensual and puritanical, is contradictory, is to be feared. It is also concrete, and is to do with women, and since cultural battles are so often fought through the bodies of women, it is seized upon by politicians, columnists, feminists.... Malak Hifni Nasif [one of the pioneering feminists] wrote in 1906 that the veil was, so to speak, a red herring. Her view was that the question of the veil was only central in the debate about women's place in society because the west (personified in Egypt then by Lord Cromer) had made it so.'[4]

Veil is a major exhibition and publication that brings together the work of twenty contemporary international artists from Muslim and non-Muslim backgrounds whose work explores the symbolic significance of the veil and veiling in contemporary culture. Curated by Al-Ani and Sedira with David A. Bailey and Gilane Tawadros, this is the first project to address the question of the veil in all its complexities and ambiguities from the vantage point of contemporary visual art practice. Just as, in recent years, there has been a trend in contemporary visual arts to re-examine the representation of the Other in art and popular culture, a number of contemporary practitioners, generally – but not exclusively – with connections to the Middle East and North Africa or other parts of the Muslim world, are producing a growing body of work that addresses the representation of the veil.

Despite the abundance of academic work which explores Orientalism as a system of knowledge and belief, a structure by which Europe illustrates its cultural and political superiority over the Orient, little has been done in exploring the particular representation of the veil in historical and contemporary visual art. And yet, no single item of clothing has had more influence on Western images of Middle Eastern and North African

Introduction
David A. Bailey and
Gilane Tawadros

women than the veil. For the first time in the history of curatorial and exhibition practice, this project extends the possible interpretations of the veil and explores the ambiguities articulated in recent and contemporary practice rather than presenting a polemical or academic thesis.

The strength and uniqueness of this project lie within the curatorial narrative which repositions the exhibition from the arena of ethnographic survey shows into a contemporary art context with a collaborative team of curators comprising artists, writers and curators. *Veil* takes up the challenge set by the 'Orientalist re-imagined' shows of the 1980s and 1990s, which were weighed down by the burden of representation, and succeeds in producing a contemporary narrative which focuses instead on the work and its relationship to twenty-first-century visual art production. Work by artists using photography, film, sculpture and mixed media – in a variety of installation practices – will be juxtaposed to comment and take a 'spin' on the theme of veil and veiling. For example, the 1960s works of documentary film-maker Gillo Pontecorvo and photographer Marc Garanger – exploring history and contested spaces in their different approaches to the Algerian War – are shown alongside the mixed-media drawings of Emily Jacir and Ghazel's video monographs which develop the idea of recovering histories within what is now seen as the transient spaces that we all occupy in our globalised world.

Orientalism, Edward Said and 'Imaginative Geographies'

Edward Said's hugely influential text *Orientalism*, first published in 1978, challenged established Western attitudes to the East and defined Orientalism as a system of knowledge about the Orient, 'an accepted grid for filtering through the Orient into Western consciousness'.[5] Importantly, Said's thesis stressed the emergence of Orientalism from the cultural hegemony of the West in relation to the East, describing Orientalism as the product of 'imaginative geography and history', a creative fiction that presented itself as reality.

According to Said, the keynote for this relationship was the French invasion of Egypt in 1798. Napoleon's flagship, the Orient, brought in its train not only an armada of ships, frigates and transports but an army of savants, a literal academy of Oriental specialists who would both aid him to conquer Egypt through their knowledge of the Orient and build what Said describes as a 'sort of living archive' for the expedition. In 1802, Napoleon commissioned the Imperial Press to begin publication of a volume on the cultural and scientific spoils of the Egyptian expedition. Four hundred copper engravers worked for twenty years on *Description de l'Egypte*, a complete visual and textual record of Egypt at the time of the expedition, not only of its antiquities but also an inventory of its flora and fauna, including 837 copper engravings and more than three thousand illustrations.

At the heart of Napoleon's project was the visual illustration of the Orient, its detailed tabulation by visual artists with the object of making it 'totally accessible to European scrutiny'.[6] While *Orientalism* relies almost entirely on literary and textual references, other writers have subsequently applied Said's thesis to the field of visual representation. Their texts articulate an unambiguous polarity between the West and the East, where the East is penetrated by the unrelenting gaze of Western eyes, leaving her (the East is always, it seems, described as female) both passive and mute. In *The Colonial Harem*, Malek Alloula subjects to scrutiny picture postcards of Algerian women produced and sent by the French in Algeria in the first decades of the twentieth century. The veiled female body emerges as a recurring preoccupation of these images and, according to Alloula, defies the gaze of the French photographer.

The first thing the foreign eye catches about Algerian women is that they are concealed from sight....

The Algerian woman does not conceal herself, does not play at concealing herself. But the eye cannot catch hold of her. The opaque veil that covers her intimates clearly and simply to the photographer a refusal.... Draped in the veil that cloaks her to her ankles, the Algerian woman discourages the *scopic desire* (the voyeurism) of the photographer. She is the concrete negation of this desire and thus brings to the photographer confirmation of a triple rejection: the rejection of his desire, of the practice of his "art," and of his place in a milieu that is not his own.[7]

How then does one read the work of Gaëtan de Clérambault? Born in France in 1872, Clérambault trained as a psychiatrist and was fascinated by the relationship between women and fabric. As a photographer, he went on to extend his research by taking images of veiled women – and occasionally men – in Morocco. He became increasingly obsessed by the drapes and forms created by the veil and the 'invisible gaze' of the veiled women he photographed, producing a huge body of photographs some of which are now in the collection of the Musée de l'Homme in Paris. But Clérambault's photographs, taken between 1918 and 1934, defy a straightforward Orientalist reading. The fact that they are not texts, but visual images without the particular historical and social context of the French postcards of Alloula's study, makes it more difficult to fix these images uniquely within an Orientalist discourse. However, Clérambault's images clearly do emerge from the same discursive field as Alloula's postcards and the images have come into being as a result of the particular colonial relationship between France and Morocco.

The female figure remains anonymous and emblematic of the exotic Middle Eastern woman and yet Clérambault's images are not presented as attempts to render his subjects accessible or transparent. They are more equivocal visual experiments in the human figure. In some, the figure is set against a neutral ground, wrapped in fabric to create different shapes. In others, the figure is set against the architecture of a domestic space, where the undulating folds of white fabric contrast against the symmetrical abstract patterns of the tiles beneath her. Unlike Alloula's postcards, the veiled figure in Clérambault's photographs is never unveiled; nor is she passive or immobile. From one image to the next, she moves and shifts, re-arranging the contours of her figure and Clérambault's composition.

By comparison with Clérambault's small-scale photographs, Kourush Adim's black and white photographic landscapes appear monumental. In place of intimate, domestic interiors, Adim's ghostly, veiled presence haunts an empty, rural landscape. A vast swathe of fabric unfolds in the wind, dwarfing its unpopulated surroundings. Located somewhere between absence and presence, figuration and abstraction, Adim's poetic photographs posit the veil as an integral part of the physical and psychological landscape. These images are far removed from a simplistic, anthropological representation of the veil that all too often presents the veil as a cipher for female oppression. For Adim, the veil becomes a constantly moving, structural feature of the natural landscape.

Architecture, Space and Modernity

In October 1910, Henri Matisse visited Munich to see the first ever international exhibition of Islamic art. An extraordinary exhibition which brought together over 3,500 objects from Islamic cultures all over the world, it had a profound effect on the direction of

Henri Matisse, *Woman with a Veil*, 1927. Oil on canvas, 61.5 x 50.2cm. The Museum of Modern Art, New York, The William S. Paley Collection. © Succession H. Matisse/DACS 2002. Digital image © 2002, The Museum of Modern Art, New York.

Matisse's work from that point on. In Clérambault's photographs, there are intimations of the challenge to traditional Western artistic practice contained within an Islamic worldview. In place of the literal representation of the human figure and the material world that had dominated classical Western representation for over five hundred years, Islamic art opened up the possibilities of abstraction, of colour fields and of radically different relationships between form and content. Most importantly, perhaps, Islamic art opened up a space for artistic expression that did not rely upon the literal presence of the human figure to articulate existential or divine ideas. In the same way that African sculpture offered avant-garde artists a new mode of seeing, Islamic art suggested ways of breaking free from the constraints of established Western traditions. This is not the place to discuss at length the extent of modernism's debt to Islamic art. Suffice to say that the dialogue and exchange between Islamic and non-Islamic cultures has had a profound effect on the way that we articulate our ideas through visual forms of representation, from painting, photography and sculpture through to architecture and gardening.

The relationship between the human figure and space and, more particularly, between the individual and the space that they occupy – both cultural and physical – is a constant theme in the work of many artists in this exhibition. For example, in Ramesh Kalkur's photographs, the line between figuration and abstraction, between photography and sculpture, is broached. Working against the grain of traditional portrait photography, Kalkur's portraits contravene its conventions by portraying individuals with their identities masked. Making identification impossible, Kalkur's portraits confound the expectations of the viewer, privileging the multiplicity of human gestures over and above the fetishisation of individual identity. The figures that populate Kalkur's portraits are concealed beneath a double veil – the fabric veil or mask that covers their face, and their hands which guard their faces from the penetration of the photographer's gaze. Kalkur's elegant images seem to suggest that there are aspects of our existence which lie beyond literal representation.

Contingent upon any discussion or exploration of the veil or veiled subject is the cultural and social demarcation of public and private space. As Malek Alloula writes, 'the veil has another function: to recall, in individualized fashion, the closure of private space. It signifies an injunction of no trespassing upon this space and it extends to another space, the one in which the photographer is to be found: public space.'[8] But the veil, like its architectural equivalent, the *mashrabiyya* (an ornate wooden screen which is a feature of traditional North African domestic architecture), operates in two directions. While it demarcates the line between public and private space,

Freya Stark, *A Street in Kuwait*, 1937. Kuwait Album, no. 19, Freya Stark Collection, Middle East Centre Photo Archive. By kind permission of the Middle East Centre, St Antony's College, Oxford.

it does not multilaterally impede the flow of light, air or vision. As Hamid Naficy writes in his essay on the poetics and politics of the veil in post-revolutionary Iranian cinema: 'Veiling as a social practice is not fixed or unidirectional; instead, it is a dynamic practice in which both men and women are implicated. In addition, there is a dialectical relationship between veiling and unveiling: that which covers is also capable of uncovering.... Veiling, therefore is not a panoptic process in the manner Foucault describes because vision is not in the possession of only one side; women and men organise the field of vision of the other.'[9]

The relationship between the veil or *mashrabiyya* and the gaze is a constant trope not only in cinema and architecture but equally in literature. Desire is eloquently articulated through the gaze in a sensual passage in Naguib Mahfouz's *Palace Walk* where one of the female protagonists, Aisha, watches the man with whom she has fallen in love through the *mashrabiyya*. They first catch sight of each other through an open window, after which Aisha returns to the *mashrabiyya* every day.

At the same hour the next day and for days after, she had gone to stand by the slit, where he could not see her. She would observe with triumphant happiness how he looked up at the closed window with concern and longing and then how his features were illumined by the light of joy as he began to discern her figure at the crack. Her heart, on fire and reaching out, awake for the first time, looked forward impatiently to this moment, savouring it happily and then dreamily bidding it adieu as it ended.[10]

Through the *mashrabiyya*, it is Aisha who controls the gaze so that, far from rendering her passive or invisible, the *mashrabiyya* in fact enables Aisha not only to manage her lover's gaze but also to communicate her feelings for him. Being veiled does not equate with being silenced, as Hamid Naficy notes in his discussion of the film *Banu-ye Ordibehesht*,[11] where the voices of two lovers circumvent the stringent rules of Iranian film censors on what can be visually portrayed on screen. The Arab diva Umm Kalthoum (who began her career reciting the Quran and singing religious songs) proved this point with her love songs which – backed by an orchestra comprising Western and Middle Eastern instruments producing Arab tonal forms – were full of intense longing and passion.

In architectural terms, the *mashrabiyya* appears simply to separate private, interior space from public, exterior space. But it ingeniously combines functional needs with cultural needs, making it an essential component in the architecture of the groundbreaking Egyptian architect Hassan Fathy. As his biographer James Steele explains, the *mashrabiyya* evolved from 'a simple, flat, perforated wooden screen into an elegant, bracketed projection, which would allow its occupants to sit inside'.

Traditionally used on both the outer and inner walls of the houses in the past, its primary social function was to prevent the women of the family from being seen by strangers, by providing a screen that would allow them to look down into the street below, or into the courtyard, or *qa'a* from the floor above without being seen. It therefore became an architectural expression of a cultural necessity.... The screens, in addition to providing privacy, cutting down glare and allowing natural ventilation, also had hygroscopic properties: the wooden balusters retain humidity of the air that passes through them. On every level, the *mashrabiya* proves, as Fathy states, that 'culture is the unique human response of man to his environment in his attempt to answer both physical and spiritual needs.'[12]

Photograph of a *mashrabiyya*,
reproduced in James Steele,
*An Architecture for People:
The Complete Works of Hassan
Fathy* (London: Thames &
Hudson, 1997). Photograph
by permission of Abdel Wahed
el-Wakil/James Steele.

Henna Nadeem, *Screen* (detail), 1997. Steel gate and railings, 3 x 13.5m. Photograph: Henna Nadeem. Nadeem combines technology and traditional Islamic geometric patterns to create a *mashrabiyya* effect on Brick Lane, an area of London with a significant Muslim community.

Above and below:
Samta Benyahia, *Nuit du Destin* (Night of Destiny), 2000. Exhibition installation, *Paris pour Escale*, Le Musée d'Art Moderne de la Ville de Paris. Photographs: Edouard Nono.

Samta Benyahia's early black and white portraits of ordinary Algerian women are enlarged to a monumental scale, filling the entire space of the gallery with their huge presence. Her recent works are embedded into the physical structure of the gallery. Laid across glass windows or doors, Benyahia's vinyl abstract designs create a contemporary *mashrabiyya* inserted into the fabric of the interior space of the building. Falling like a physical veil across the viewer's line of vision, Benyahia's installations designate different spatial zones, demarcating new public and private spaces within the gallery. With Benyahia's abstract patterns in place, it is impossible to see the space unmediated. A veil has been drawn by the artist that makes us acutely conscious of the precise delineations of spaces. It also makes us profoundly aware of the process of seeing and its myriad mediations. Is it possible, asks Benyahia, to see the world without the screen of social and cultural assumptions?

Photography, Veiling and the Politics of Representation

In her essay 'Visibility, Violence, and Voice? Attitudes to Veiling Post-11 September', Alison Donnell argues that there has been a decisive shift, a quantum leap even, in attitudes to veiling since 11 September, after which time the veil became a symbol of oppression in Western eyes.

> The familiar and much-analysed Orientalist gaze through which the veil is viewed as an object of mystique, exoticism and eroticism and the veiled woman as an object of fantasy, excitement and desire is now replaced by the xenophobic, more specifically Islamophobic, gaze through which the veil, or headscarf, is seen as a highly visible sign of a despised difference.... Post-11 September, it

would appear that attitudes to and representations of the veil have overwhelmingly demonstrated the intransigence of the veiled woman as an icon of oppression – an embodiment of the rationale for the continuation of George W. Bush's war without end, a strategic figure constantly evoked as a visual reminder of the incommensurability between Western and Islamic societies.[13]

It is precisely the incommensurability between Western and Islamic societies so prevalent in the media that is invoked by AES art group's provocative digitally manipulated photographs. The image of the veiled Statue of Liberty or that of Muslims massing on a Western metropolis visualise the deep-seated Islamophobia of which Donnell writes and its constant reiteration through images in film, television and photography. How does one begin to deconstruct the barrage of mediated images and strip away culturally reinforced prejudices?

The works of both the artists' collective AES and Mitra Tabrizian engage with the role of photography in mediating and, not infrequently, manipulating lived experiences. Mitra Tabrizian's black and white billboard image *Surveillance* (1990) engages with the icon of the veiled woman once again, but this time from the vantage point of post-revolutionary Iran where she is emblematic not of 'despised difference' but of the victory of Islamic values over Western values. A key player in the early debates on photography and representation in the 1980s, Tabrizian's panoramic photograph suggests the power of photography and media representation to take on the authority of historical authenticity and documentary evidence.

The exploration of genres within photography and painting in order to narrativise questions of representation is also central to the work of Faisal Abdu'Allah. In the artist's own words:

'My work is not there so that voyeurs can look down on people they believe to be in a lesser state than themselves. My work is about us looking at ourselves through people with a certain degree of power and presence.'[14] Although *The Last Supper* (1995) makes reference to the European discourse in painting, Abdu'Allah represents a new generation of black artists in Britain who are exploring geographical and cultural links with black America and Africa. For Abdu'Allah, this large-scale photographic work is a hybridised canvas which reworks and rehistoricises the figure of the Nubian Messiah. The repetitious use of the black male figure alludes to Abdu'Allah's earlier work on the racial coding of black masculinity within a modern aesthetic and to the black diasporic figure in contemporary photography. Meanwhile the scale of the work and richness of its photographic quality (archival selenium-toned bromide print) seduce the viewer in their play on advertising billboard imagery within popular culture.

Farah Bajull's thirty-metre long string of handmade, oversized worry beads – made of wood and wound tightly into a ball – forms part of her installation *Notime* (2001). Adjacent to the wound ball of worry beads on the floor, a photograph of a woman seated and bound by the string of worry beads hangs on the wall. The intricate knot seems to symbolise the intractability of the problem of bridging cultural and religious differences against the current of the continuous stream of media images which caricature and steadily reinforce the idea of unbridgeable, irreconcilable difference between Western and Islamic societies. The anonymous woman is apparently held, trapped by this enforced divide.

In Ghazel's series of video diaries, *Me* (1997–2000), the artist films herself undertaking a variety of pursuits – skate-boarding, boxing, taking a ballet lesson or sheltering during an air raid – fully attired in a chador. Shot in Iran, Paris, Montpellier and New York, Ghazel's comic and sometimes absurd films, attest to the banality of difference, making the artist – who plays herself – both the comic subject and at the same time irrelevant prop in her biographical mini-features. In Ghazel's world, the veil is a feature of everyday life.

Shadafarin Ghadirian's pastiches of traditional studio photography provide a humorous reflection upon the impact of cultural and technological traffic that exists between Iran and the West. Inspired by the portraits of the Qajar dynasty (1785–1925), Ghadirian recreated a Qajar studio in her Tehran home. She scrupulously choreographed the formal poses, then added ghetto blasters, televisions, vacuum cleaners and bicycles. Studio photography became established in the Middle East in the nineteenth century in the footsteps of European travellers who used the new technology of the photographic camera to record their travels. Ghadirian's ironic black and white portraits document the latest stage of cultural and technological exchange in the new global economy, precisely tabulating social and cultural mores in contemporary Iran.

A comic Buster Keaton-like sensibility permeates the work of Harold Offeh. His video piece *Alien Communication* (1999), like other of Offeh's works, is a humorous but troubling exploration of the politics of representation. A large magnifying glass, synonymous with scientific investigation, distorts the artist's face, blowing it up to surreal proportions. Using comic everyday scenes of frustration and alienation, Offeh presents a reality that is veiled or distorted through the use of a variety of photographic techniques. Offeh's work can be seen as a wry commentary on the disfiguring effects of media representations of racial and ethnic difference where the photographic lens wilfully distorts reality. And it is as a cipher for unequivocal, uncompromising difference that the image of the veil permeates Western society.

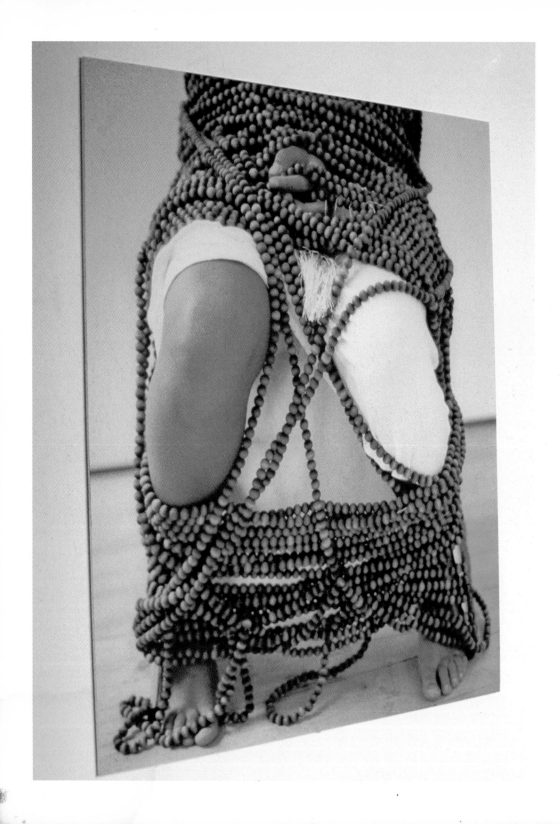

Farah Bajull, *Notime* (detail),
2001. Digital print, 76 x 61cm.
Photograph: Lee Funnell.

Farah Bajull, *Notime* (detail),
2001. Worry beads and string,
29cm diameter. Photograph:
Lee Funnell.

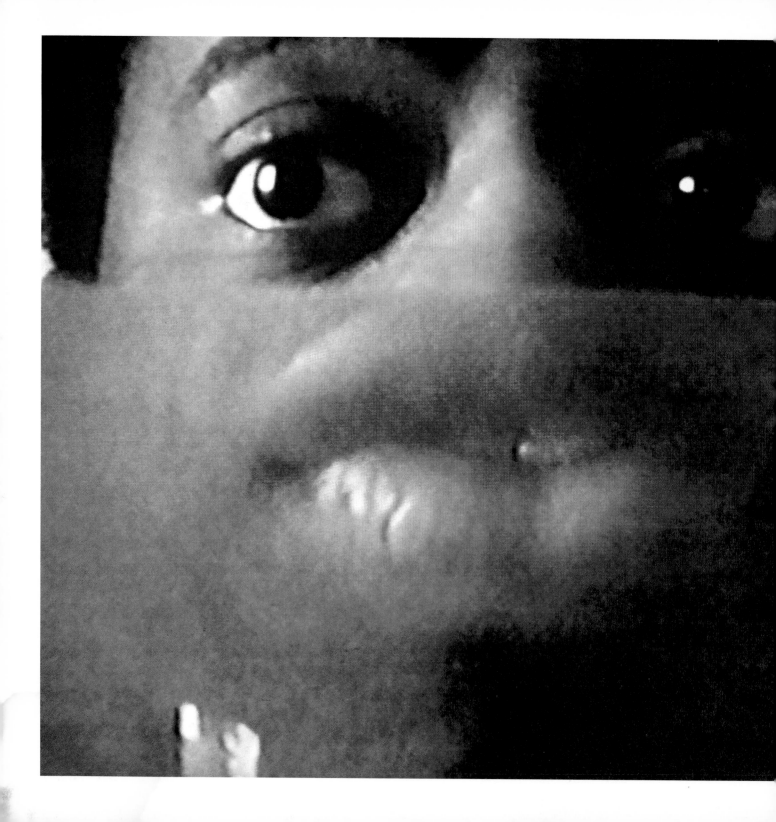

Harold Offeh, *Alien Communication*, 1999. Video projection, 5 mins.

Robert Mapplethorpe, *Lisa Lyon*, 1982. © The Estate of Robert Mapplethorpe. Used with permission. Mapplethorpe's image of bodybuilder Lisa Lyon tests accepted boundaries for the depiction of the female body.

Veiling the Body: Sexuality, Censorship and Cultural Difference

The Western [sic] word *veil* is "sexy" and marketable in the West. It thus tends to be overused, invariably out of or without context, in titles of books, articles, conferences, press, films and popular literature in a way disproportionate to the relative significance of the veil in Middle Eastern affairs, and irrespective of the quality of knowledge about the veil. Some scholars of Islam have expressed concern that "veil" has come to replace "crescent" as a symbol of Islam in the West, which is outrageous. Rather, the veil has come to replace the earlier obsession with "harems" and *hammams*. "Harems" and *hammams* then and the "veil" now evoke a public sexual energy that early Christianity, puritanist Western culture, and contemporary elements of fundamentalist Christianity have not been able to come to terms with, comprehend or tolerate. In the West *harem*, *veil*, *polygamy* invoke Islam and are synonymous with female weakness and oppression.[15]

Emily Jacir's installation is made up of numerous drawings on tracing paper, inspired by a memory from her childhood. She recalls her mother, on the airplane home to Saudi Arabia after a trip abroad, blocking out the uncovered arms and legs of the models in her fashion magazine with black felt pen. *From Paris to Riyadh* (1998–2001) is a large-scale, black and white wall installation, made up of seemingly abstract drawings on tracing paper. The forms of female figures move across the expanse, their black limbs standing out in stark contrast to the field of white surrounding them. The outlines of the models' bodies slip in and out of view, dissolving into abstract geometric shapes and then re-emerging as human figures, playing on the border between abstraction and figuration.

Abstraction and figuration, absence and presence, are also themes in Ghada Amer's work. At first glance and from a distance, Amer's works appear to be finely drawn, abstract and spontaneous, like automatist drawings on canvas. On closer inspection, one actually discovers that they are in fact fragmented lines of figurative embroidery, describing the naked or scantily clad female body in the archetypal poses of pornography. With *Majnun* (1997), Amer has roughly stitched words on to the fabric of a closet. The work makes reference to the story of the character Majnun, equivalent to Romeo in the literature of the Islamic world, who is driven mad by his unrequited love. Written in French, the text of Amer's work attests to the convergence of love and death in the language of a love letter or poem. Invoking the world of hidden love,

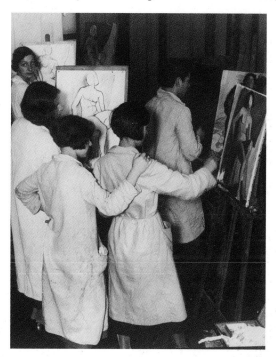

From Veiled Women to Life Classes with Nude Models, Turkey. Published in *National Geographic Magazine*, January 1939. Photograph: Lubinski, Kurt & Margot, courtesy of the National Geographic Image Collection.

Following Ataturk's sweeping modernisation reforms, which included a campaign against the veiling of women, these women were able to study life drawing.

Amer's installation *Majnun* (which means 'mad' in Arabic) simultaneously makes visible the linguistic but veils the physical from view.

Drapery and sexuality are key motifs in Elin Strand's work. In her performance piece, *Speaking Bernina* (2000), swathes of fabric envelop the performers who patiently stitch themselves into the metres of drapery which ebb and flow around their bodies like waves on the ocean. Concerned with questions of concealment and sexual identity, Strand's work explores the ways in which sexual restrictions and conventions censure and veil our individuality.

In a similar vein to Faisal Abdu'Allah, Majida Khattari appropriates advertising codes to produce sculptural performance pieces that address adornment within the practice of live art. On the surface, these works appear to play on Gap and Benetton advertisements, but, in fact, Khattari is targeting fashion conglomerates and the fashion world to produce 'animated fabric objects' where the so-called catwalk takes central stage as an artistic performance piece. In these staged events, the performers, how they are dressed and how they address the audience are all central to understanding the work. For instance, in an earlier series, Khattari draped one of her performers with a garment embroidered with the Coca-Cola logo in the style of Islamic calligraphy, as a play on the performer, the product, corporate iconography and language.

In very different ways, the works of Strand, Amer, Khattari and Jacir disrupt the simplistic binaries that are repeatedly invoked about the liberal West and censorious East and reflect upon the myriad ways in which female sexuality continues to occupy our collective imaginations. But, as Leila Ahmed points out, the continuous reiteration of the veil and veiling as a site of struggle and contestation about the position of women in Islam over the decades has concealed a more fundamental struggle from view, namely the historical struggle for national self-determination in opposition to colonialism.

Because of this history of struggle around it, the veil is now pregnant with meanings... [a] legacy of meanings and struggles over issues of culture and class with which not only the veil but also the struggle for women's rights as a whole has become inscribed as a result of this history and as a result of the cooptation by colonialism of the issue of women and the language of feminism in its attempt to undermine other cultures....

To a considerable extent, overtly or covertly, inadvertently or otherwise, discussions of women in Islam in academies and outside them, and in Muslim countries and outside them, continue either to reinscribe the Western narrative of Islam as oppressor and the West as liberator and native classist versions of that narrative or, conversely, to reinscribe the contentions of the Arabic narrative of resistance as to the essentialness of preserving Muslim customs, particularly with regard to women, as a sign of resistance to imperialism, whether colonial or postcolonial.[16]

Women, History and the Veil

In an early interview, when asked what she thought about women and the veil, the artist Shirin Neshat responded:

From the beginning I made a decision that [my photographic] work was not going to be about me or my opinion on the subject, and that my position was going to be no position. I then put myself at a place of only asking questions but never answering them. The main question and curiosity was simply being a woman in Islam. I then decided to put the trust in those women's words who had lived and experienced the life of a woman behind a veil. So each time I inscribed a specific women's writings on my photographs, the work took a new direction.[17]

In Neshat's photographic pieces selected for the exhibition – *Allegiance with Wakefulness* (1994), *The Rebellious Silence* from the *Women of Allah* series (1994), *Shameless* (1997) and *I Am Its Secret* (1999) – the layering of text, the image of the gun, the facial representations and the blackened veil suggest that the photographic frame becomes a site where images compete with each other. Such contestation relates to the idea of the body becoming a battleground for visual languages and political discourse, a dilemma to which the artist provides no resolution. The interplay between the subject and viewer – with the veil and gun serving as props – suggests that these photographic works are framed as performance pieces in much the same way as Majida Khattari uses adornment to frame her performative works. In some ways, Neshat's works can be seen as protagonists entering the stage on which the veil and veiling have been embroiled in the history of the struggle against colonialism and, more recently, neo-colonialism. And, as Jananne Al-Ani's poetic projection piece *Veil* (1997) suggests, historical narrative is a differently articulated and fragmented activity made up of an assemblage of individual experiences. As the camera fixes each one in its view like a formal studio portrait, five women of different ages appear veiled, unveiled and re-veiled to different degrees, over and over again.

It is hard to extricate the veil from this history since, as Leila Ahmed points out, the discourses of feminism, of colonialism and of indigenous resistance gradually became deeply intertwined. Huda Sha'rawi's ceremonial public unveiling in 1923 on her return from a feminist meeting in Rome is seen by Ahmed as evidence of the degree to which Sha'rawi as an upper-class Egyptian had uncritically taken on board Western cultural values and yet, only four years earlier, Sha'rawi had become deeply involved in the nationalist struggle against British occupation, leading demonstrations of women. Her public gesture of unveiling, however, has eclipsed her political activism and resistance to colonialism which sits uncomfortably within a homogeneous narrative of feminist struggle.

We women held our first demonstration on 16 March to protest the repressive acts and intimidation practised by the British authority. In compliance with the orders of the authority we announced our plans to demonstrate in advance but were refused permission.... On the morning of the 16th, I sent placards to the house of Ahmad Bey Abu Usbaa, bearing slogans in Arabic and French painted in white on a background of black – the colour of mourning. Some of the slogans read, 'Long Live the Supporters of Justice and Freedom', others said 'Down with Oppressors and Tyrants', and 'Down with Occupation'.[18]

The Martiniquan psychoanalyst Frantz Fanon has written at length of the psychological and socio-political dynamic of colonialism and its impact on both colonisers and colonised. In his compelling study of the Algerian Revolution, he identifies the 'historical dynamism of the veil' in the development of colonisation and native resistance with the *unveiling* of Algeria as a nation.

In the beginning, the veil was a mechanism of resistance but its value for the social group remained very strong. The veil was worn because tradition demanded a rigid separation of the sexes, but also because the occupier *was bent on unveiling Algeria*. In a second phase, the mutation

Elin Strand, *Speaking Bernina,*
October 2000.
Four day performance at the
Pump House Gallery, London.
Photographs: Elin Strand.

occurred in connection with the Revolution and under special circumstances. The veil was abandoned in the course of revolutionary action. What had been used to block the psychological or political offensives of the occupier became a means, an instrument. The veil helped the Algerian woman to meet the new problems created by the struggle.[19]

Two more or less contemporary but very different 'documents' of the period reveal the symbolic and physical significance of the veil in the colonial struggle over Algeria: Gillo Pontecorvo's film *Battle of Algiers* (1965) and Marc Garanger's black and white portraits of unveiled Algerian women from 1960. Pontecorvo's landmark film employed the genre of the black and white documentary film to powerful effect in his fictional restaging of the *Battle of Algiers*. Pontecorvo presents veiling as a tool of resistance deployed by Algerian women against their French colonial occupiers. In one memorable scene, an Algerian woman conceals a gun beneath her clothes and then dresses to cover her body and face before going outside and passing through a French military checkpoint. Pontecorvo's work echoes the ideas of Fanon: 'I cannot go to a film without seeing myself. I wait for me. The people in the theatre are watching me, examining me, waiting for me.'[20] For Pontecorvo and Fanon the theatrical space of cinema becomes the site of subjection to a complex bombardment of images, looks and ideologies which disorientate our subjectivities and identities. Hence, the *Battle of Algiers* explores not only the battle for Algerian independence, but also the battle of images. The film is now seen as a template that illustrates the fusing of the fictive with the documentary in its use of a black and white neorealist style and its adoption of the film noir flashback technique. Pontecorvo's reconstruction of historical events is a theme taken up and developed further by other artists in the exhibition, as we see in the photographic panoramic work of Mitra Tabrizian and Faisal Abdu'Allah.

It is the process of unveiling rather than veiling that lies behind Garanger's disturbing portraits of Algerian women. Compelled by his commander to unveil Algerian women by force and take their photographs for identification purposes, Garanger, who was working as a military photographer at the time, described his superior's attitude to his assignment as an obscene physical attack, a kind of rape. He believed that this rape was not the first that the Algerian women had suffered; the first rape was the unveiling itself.

In Zineb Sedira's mesmerising video *Silent Sight* (2000), the kohl-rimmed eyes of a woman stare out through a rectangular strip, framed by a white veil. Her eyes open and close. They blink. They look to the right and then to the left. Here, it is the woman's gaze and the control of her own gaze that takes precedence, while the veil dissolves into a white haze. Discussing the colonial photographer's reading of the veil, Alloula writes: 'The whiteness of the veil becomes the symbolic equivalent of blindness: leukoma, a white speck on the eye of the photographer and his viewfinder. *Whiteness is the absence of a photo, a veiled photograph, a whiteout, in technical terms.* From its background nothing emerges except some vague contours, anonymous in their repeated resemblance. Nothing distinguishes one veiled woman from another.'[21] By contrast to this colonial 'blindness', the artists, writers and film-makers in this project present a myriad different ways of seeing and reading the veil. Insisting on its diversity and complexity, *Veil* opens up a space for dialogue and exchange about the varied social, cultural and historical meanings of the veil through the prism of contemporary visual arts practice.

Notes

1. For a comprehensive study of the veil, see Fadwa El Guindi's excellent *Veil: Modesty, Privacy and Resistance*. New York and Oxford: Berg, 1999.

2. Al-Ani, Jananne. 'Acting Out', see p. 106.

3. Sedira, Zineb. 'Mapping the Illusive', see pp. 58–63.

4. Soueif, Ahdaf. 'The Language of the Veil', see pp. 110 and 113.

5. Said, Edward. *Orientalism*. London: Peregrine Books, rev. ed., 1985, p. 6.

6. Ibid, p. 83.

7. Alloula, Malek. *The Colonial Harem*. Manchester: Manchester University Press, 1987, p. 7.

8. Ibid, p. 13.

9. Naficy, Hamid. 'Poetics and Politics of the Veil, Voice and Vision in Iranian Post-revolutionary Cinema', see p. 140.

10. Mahfouz, Naguib. *Palace Walk*. London: Doubleday, 1990, p. 25.

11. Naficy, Hamid, op. cit., see p. 152.

12. Steele, James. *An Architecture for People: The Complete Works of Hassan Fathy*. London: Thames & Hudson, 1997, p. 85.

13. Donnell, Alison. 'Visibility, Violence and Voice? Attitudes to Veiling Post-11 September', see pp. 122–23 and 134.

14. Interview with Faisal Abdu'Allah, *The Face*, issue no. 58, 1993.

15. El Guindi, Fadwa, op. cit., p. 10.

16. Ahmed, Leila. *Women and Gender in Islam*, New Haven and London: Yale University Press, 1992, pp. 166–67.

17. Interview with Lina Bertucci, 'Shirin Neshat: Eastern Values', *Flash Art*, November-December, 1997, pp. 84–86.

18. Sha'rawi, Huda. *Harem Years: The Memoirs of an Egyptian Feminist*, translated and introduced by Margot Badran, London: Virago Press, 1986, p. 113.

19. Fanon, Frantz. *Studies in a Dying Colonialism*, rev. ed., London: Earthscan Publications, 1989, p. 63.

20. Fanon, Frantz. *Black Skin, White Masks*. London: Pluto Press, 1980.

21. Alloula, Malek, op. cit., p. 7.

The Discourse of the Veil
Leila Ahmed

Qassim Amin's *Tahrir Al-Mar'a* (The Liberation of Woman), published in 1899, during a time of visible social change and lively intellectual ferment, caused intense and furious debate. Analyses of the debate and of the barrage of opposition the book provoked have generally assumed that it was the radicalness of Amin's proposals with respect to women that caused the furore. Yet the principal substantive recommendations that Amin advocated for women – giving them a primary-school education and reforming the laws on polygamy and divorce – could scarcely be described as innovatory.... Muslim intellectuals such as al-Tahtawi and 'Abdu had argued for women's education and called for reforms in matters of polygamy and divorce in the 1870s and 1880s and even earlier without provoking violent controversy. Indeed, by the 1890s the issue of educating women not only to the primary level but beyond was so uncontroversial that both state and Muslim benevolent societies had established girls' schools.

The anger and passion Amin's work provoked becomes intelligible only when one considers not the substantive reforms for women that he advocated but rather, first, the symbolic reform – the abolition of the veil – that he passionately urged and, second, the reforms, indeed the fundamental changes in culture and society, that he urged upon society as a whole and that he contended it was essential for the Egyptian nation, and Muslim countries generally, to make. The need for a general cultural and social transformation is the central thesis of the book, and it is within this thesis that the arguments regarding women are embedded: changing customs regarding women and changing their costume, abolishing the veil in particular, were key, in the author's thesis, to bringing about the desired general social transformation. Examining how Amin's recommendations regarding women formed part of his general thesis and how and why he believed that unveiling was the key to social transformations

is essential to unraveling the significance of the debate that his book provoked.

Amin's work has traditionally been regarded as marking the beginning of feminism in Arab culture. Its publication and the ensuing debate certainly constitute an important moment in the history of Arab women: the first battle of the veil to agitate the Arab press. The battle inaugurated a new discourse in which the veil came to comprehend significations far broader than merely the position of women. Its connotations now encompassed issues of class and culture – the widening cultural gulf between the different classes in society and the interconnected conflict between the culture of the colonizers and that of the colonized. It was in this discourse, too, that the issues of women and culture first appeared as inextricably fused in Arabic discourse. Both the key features of this new discourse, the greatly expanded signification of the veil and the fusion of the issues of women and culture, that made their formal entry into Arab discourse with the publication of Amin's work had their provenance in the discourses of European societies. In Egypt the British colonial presence and discursive input constituted critical components in the situation that witnessed the emergence of the new discourse of the veil....

The colonial presence and the colonizer's economic and political agenda, plus the role that cultural training and affiliation played in widening the gap between classes, provided ample ground for the emergence at this moment of the issue of culture as fraught and controversial. Why the contest over culture should center on women and the veil and why Amin fastened upon those issues as the key to cultural and social transformation only becomes intelligible, however, by reference to ideas imported into the local situation from the colonizing society. Those ideas were interjected into the native discourse as Muslim men exposed to European ideas began to reproduce and react to them and, subsequently and more pervasively

The Discourse of the Veil
Leila Ahmed

and insistently, as Europeans – servants of empire and individuals resident in Egypt – introduced and actively disseminated them.....

Broadly speaking, the thesis of the discourse on Islam blending a colonialism committed to male dominance with feminism – the thesis of the new colonial discourse of Islam centered on women – was that Islam was innately and immutably oppressive to women, that the veil and segregation epitomized that oppression, and that these customs were the fundamental reasons for the general and comprehensive backwardness of Islamic societies. Only if these practices "intrinsic" to Islam (and therefore Islam itself) were cast off could Muslim societies begin to move forward on the path of civilization. Veiling – to *Western* eyes, the most visible marker of the differentness and inferiority of Islamic societies – became the symbol now of both the oppression of women (or, in the language of the day, Islam's degradation of women) and the backwardness of Islam, and it became the open target of colonial attack and the spearhead of the assault on Muslim societies....

That the Victorian colonial paternalistic establishment appropriated the language of feminism in the service of its assault on the religions and cultures of Other men, and in particular on Islam, in order to give an aura of moral justification to that assault at the very same time as it combated feminism within its own society can easily be substantiated by reference to the conduct and rhetoric of the colonizers. The activities of Lord Cromer are particularly illuminating on the subject, perfectly exemplifying how, when it came to the cultures of other men, white supremacist views, androcentric and paternalistic convictions, and feminism came together in harmonious and actually entirely logical accord in the service of the imperial idea.

Cromer had quite decided views on Islam, women in Islam, and the veil. He believed quite simply that Islamic religion and society were inferior to the European ones and bred inferior men. The inferiority of the men was evident in numerous ways, which Cromer lists at length. ...

Whereas Christianity teaches respect for women, and European men "elevated" women because of the teachings of their religion, Islam degraded them, Cromer wrote, and it was to this degradation, most evident in the practices of veiling and segregation, that the inferiority of Muslim men could be traced. Nor could it be doubted that the practices of veiling and seclusion exercised "a baneful effect on Eastern society. The arguments in the case are, indeed, so commonplace that it is unnecessary to dwell on them."[1] It was essential that Egyptians "be persuaded or forced into imbibing the true spirit of western civilisation" (2:538), Cromer stated, and to achieve this, it was essential to change the position of women in Islam, for it was Islam's degradation of women, expressed in the practices of veiling and seclusion, that was "the fatal obstacle" to the Egyptian's "attainment of that elevation of thought and character which should accompany the introduction of Western civilisation" (2:538-39); only by abandoning those practices might they attain "the mental and moral development which he [Cromer] desired for them."[2]

Even as he delivered himself of such views, the policies Cromer pursued were detrimental to Egyptian women. The restrictions he placed on government schools and his raising of school fees held back girls'

Jananne Al-Ani, *Veil*, 1997. Still from projection installation, courtesy essor gallery.

Jananne Al-Ani, *Untitled*, 1996.
Black and white photographs,
180 x 120cm, courtesy essor
gallery.

education as well as boys'. He also discouraged the training of women doctors. Under the British, the School for Hakimas, which had given women as many years of medical training as the men received in the School of Medicine, was restricted to midwifery. On the local preference among women for being treated by women Cromer said, "I am aware that in exceptional cases women like to be attended by female doctors, but I conceive that throughout the civilised world, attendance by medical men is still the rule."[3]

However, it was in his activities in relation to women in his own country that Cromer's paternalistic convictions and his belief in the proper subordination of women most clearly declared themselves. This champion of the unveiling of Egyptian women was, in England, a founding member and sometime president of the Men's League for Opposing Women's Suffrage.[4] Feminism on the home front and feminism directed against white men was to be resisted and suppressed; but taken abroad and directed against the cultures of colonized peoples, it could be promoted in ways that admirably served and furthered the project of the dominance of the white man.

Others besides the official servants of empire promoted these kinds of ideas: missionaries, for example. For them, too, the degradation of women in Islam legitimized the attack on native culture. A speaker at a missionary conference held in London in 1888 observed that Muhammad had been exemplary as a young man but took many wives in later life and set out to preach a religion whose object was "to extinguish women altogether"; and he introduced the veil, which "has had the most terrible and injurious effect upon the mental, moral and spiritual history of all Mohammedan races." Missionary women delivered themselves of the same views. One wrote that Muslim women needed to be rescued by their Christian sisters from the "ignorance and degradation" in which they existed, and converted to Christianity.

Their plight was a consequence of the nature of their religion, which gave license to "lewdness." Marriage in Islam was "not founded on love but on sensuality," and a Muslim wife, "buried alive behind the veil," was regarded as "prisoner and slave rather than... companion and helpmeet." Missionary school teachers actively attacked the custom of veiling by seeking to persuade girls to defy their families and not wear one. For the missionaries, as for Cromer, women were the key to converting backward Muslim societies into civilized Christian societies. One missionary openly advocated targeting women, because women molded children. Islam should be undermined subtly and indirectly among the young, and when children grew older, "the evils of Islam could be spelled out more directly." Thus a trail of "gunpowder" would be laid "into the heart of Islam."[5]

Others besides officials and missionaries similarly promoted these ideas, individuals resident in Egypt, for example. Well-meaning European feminists, such as Eugénie Le Brun (who took the young Huda Sha'rawi under her wing), earnestly inducted young Muslim women into the European understanding of the meaning of the veil and the need to cast it off as the essential first step in the struggle for female liberation.

Whether such proselytizers from the West were colonial patriarchs, then, or missionaries or feminists,

Young women in Nablus, Palestine, collecting donations for the nationalist cause during the Palestine rebellion, 1937–38. Photograph published in *The Arab Woman and the Palestine Question*, the proceedings of a conference of Eastern women held in Cairo, 15–18 October 1938.

Defying the stereotype of the veiled woman as passive and oppressed, these young Palestinian women were politically active in 1937–38.

all essentially insisted that Muslims had to give up their native religion, customs, and dress, or at least reform their religion and habits along the recommended lines, and for all of them the veil and customs regarding women were the prime matters requiring reform. And all assumed their right to denounce native ways, and in particular the veil, and to set about undermining the culture in the name of whatever cause they claimed to be serving – civilizing the society, or Christianizing it, or saving women from the odious culture and religion in which they had the misfortune to find themselves....

The ideas to which Cromer and the missionaries gave expression formed the basis of Amin's book. The rationale in which Amin, a French-educated upper-middle-class lawyer, grounded his call for changing the position of women and for abolishing the veil was essentially the same as theirs. Amin's text also assumed and declared the inherent superiority of Western civilization and the inherent backwardness of Muslim societies: he wrote that anyone familiar with "the East" had observed "the backwardness of Muslims in the East wherever they are." ....

The demand that was most vehemently and widely denounced was his call for an end to segregation and veiling. Amin's arguments, like the discourse of the colonizers, are grounded in the presumption that veiling and seclusion were customs that, in Cromer's words, "exercised a baneful effect on Eastern society." The veil constituted, wrote Amin, "a huge barrier between woman and her elevation, and consequently a barrier between the nation and its advance" (54).[6] Unfortunately, his assault on the veil represented not the result of reasoned reflection and analysis but rather the internalization and replication of the colonialist perception.

Pared of rhetoric, Amin's argument against seclusion and veiling was simply that girls would forget all they had learned if they were made to veil and observe seclusion after they were educated. The age at which girls were veiled and secluded, twelve to fourteen, was a crucial age for the development of talents and intellect, and veiling and seclusion frustrated that development; girls needed to mix freely with men, for learning came from such mixing (55–56). This position is clearly not compatible with his earlier statement that anything beyond a primary-school education was "unnecessary" for girls. If intellectual development and the acquisition of knowledge were indeed important goals for women, then the rational recommendation would be to pursue these goals directly with increased schooling, not indirectly by ending segregation and veiling so that women could associate with men.

Even more specious – as well as offensive to any who did not share Amin's uncritical and wholesale respect for European man and his presumption of inferiority of native practices – was another argument he advanced for the abandonment of the veil. After asserting that veiling and seclusion were common to all societies in ancient times, he said: "Do Egyptians imagine that the men of Europe, who have attained such completeness of intellect and feeling that they were able to discover the force of steam and electricity... these souls that daily risk their lives in the pursuit of knowledge and honor above the pleasures of life... these intellects and these souls that we so admire, could possibly fail to know the means of safeguarding woman and preserving her purity? Do they think that such people would have abandoned veiling after it had been in use among them if they had seen any good in it?" (67).

In one section of the book, however, the argument against veiling is rationally made: the chapter which 'Amara suggests was composed by 'Abdu. 'Abdu points out the real disadvantages to women of segregation and veiling. These customs compel them to conduct matters of law and business through an intermediary, placing poor women, who need to earn a living in trade or domestic service, in the false and impossible position of dealing with men in a society that officially bans such dealings (47–48)....

Passages suggestive of careful thought are the exception rather than the rule in this work, however.[7] More commonly the book presented strident criticism of Muslim, particularly Egyptian, culture and society. In calling for women's liberation the thoroughly patriarchal Amin was in fact calling for the transformation of Muslim society along the lines of the Western model and for the substitution of the garb of Islamic-style male dominance for that of Western-style male dominance. Under the guise of a plea for the "liberation" of women, then, he conducted an attack that in its fundamentals reproduced the colonizer's attack on native culture and society. For Amin as for the colonizers, the veil and segregation symbolized the backwardness and inferiority of Islamic society; in his discourse as in theirs, therefore, the veil and segregation came in for the most direct attack. For Amin as for Cromer, women and their dress were important counters in the discourse concerning the relative merits of the societies and civilizations of men and their different styles of male domination; women themselves and their liberation were no more important to Amin than to Cromer.

Amin's book thus represents the rearticulation in native voice of the colonial thesis of the inferiority of the native and Muslim and the superiority of the European. Rearticulated in native upper-middle-class voice, the voice of a class economically allied with the colonizers and already adopting their life-styles, the colonialist thesis took on a classist dimension: it became in effect an attack (in addition to all the other broad and specific attacks) on the customs of the lower-middle and lower classes.

The book is reckoned to have triggered the first major controversy in the Arabic press: more than thirty books and articles appeared in response to its publication. The majority were critical, though the book did please some readers, notably members of the British administration and pro-British factions: the pro-British paper *Al-muqattam* hailed the book

as the finest in years.[8] There were evidently many reasons for Muslims and Egyptians, for nationalists of all stripes, to dislike the work: Amin's adulation of the British and of European civilization, his contempt for natives and native ways, his insulting references to the reigning family and to specific groups and classes, such as the 'ulama (who were prominent among the critics of his book), and his implied and indeed explicit contempt for the customs of the lower classes. However, just as Amin had used the issue of women and the call for their unveiling to conduct his generalized assault on society, so too did the rebuttals of his work come in the form of an affirmation of the customs that he had attacked – veiling and segregation. In a way that was to become typical of the Arabic narrative of resistance, the opposition appropriated, in order to negate them, the terms set in the first place by the colonial discourse.

Analysts routinely treat the debate as one between "feminists," that is, Amin and his allies, and "antifeminists," that is, Amin's critics. They accept at face value the equation made by Amin and the originating Western narrative: that the veil signified oppression, therefore those who called for its abandonment were feminists and those opposing its abandonment were antifeminists.[9] As I have suggested, however, the fundamental and contentious premise of Amin's work was its endorsement of the Western view of Islamic civilization, peoples, and customs as inferior, whereas the author's position on women was profoundly patriarchal and even somewhat misogynist. The book merely called for the substitution of Islamic-style male dominance by Western-style male dominance. Far from being the father of Arab feminism, then, Amin might more aptly be described as the son of Cromer and colonialism.

Opponents with a nationalist perspective were therefore not necessarily any more antifeminist than Amin was feminist. Some who defended the national custom had views on women considerably more "feminist" than Amin's, but others who opposed unveiling, for nationalist and Islamist reasons, had views on women no less patriarchal than his. For example, the attacks on Amin's book published in *Al-liwa*, Mustapha Kamil's paper, declared that women had the same right to an education as men and that their education was as essential to the nation as men's – a position considerably more liberal and feminist than Amin's. The writers opposed unveiling not as antifeminists, it seems, but as cogent analysts of the current social situation. They did not argue that veiling was immutable Islamic custom, saying, on the contrary, that future generations might decree otherwise. They argued that veiling was the current practice and that Amin's call to unveil was merely part of the hasty and unconsidered rush to imitate the West in everything.[10] This perspective anticipates an incisive and genuinely feminist analysis of the issue of the veil and the accompanying debate offered a few years later by Malak Nassef, discussed in the next chapter.

Tal'at Harb's nationalist response to Amin, in contrast, defended and upheld Islamic practices, putting forward a view of the role and duties of women in society quite as patriarchal as Amin's; but where Amin wanted to adopt a Western-style male dominance, describing his recommendation as a call for women's liberation, Harb argued for an Islamic patriarchy, presenting his views quite simply as those of traditional, unadorned, God-ordained patriarchy. Harb invoked Christian and Muslim scriptures and Western and Muslim men of learning to affirm that the wife's duty was to attend to the physical, mental, and moral needs of her husband and children[11] – the same duty that Amin ascribed to her. Their prescriptions for women differed literally in the matter of garb: Harb's women must veil, and Amin's unveil. The argument between Harb and Amin centered not on feminism versus antifeminism but on Western versus indigenous ways. For neither side was male dominance ever in question.

Amin's book, then, marks the entry of the colonial narrative of women and Islam – in which the veil and the treatment of women epitomized Islamic inferiority – into mainstream Arabic discourse. And the opposition it generated similarly marks the emergence of an Arabic narrative developed in resistance to the colonial narrative. This narrative of resistance appropriated, in order to negate them, the symbolic terms of the originating narrative. The veil came to symbolize in the resistance narrative, not the inferiority of the culture and the need to cast aside its customs in favor of those of the West, but, on the contrary, the dignity and validity of all native customs, and in particular those customs coming under fiercest colonial attack – the customs relating to women – and the need to tenaciously affirm them as a means of resistance to Western domination. As Frantz Fanon was to say of a later battle of the veil, between the French and the Algerians, the Algerians affirmed the veil because "tradition demanded the rigid separation of the sexes" and because "*the occupier was bent on unveiling Algeria*" (emphasis in original).[12] Standing in the relation of antithesis to thesis, the resistance narrative thus reversed – but thereby also accepted – the terms set in the first place by the colonizers. And therefore, ironically, it is Western discourse that in the first place determined the new meanings of the veil and gave rise to its emergence as a symbol of resistance.

Amin's book and the debate it generated, and the issues of class and culture with which the debate became inscribed, may be regarded as the precursor and prototype of the debate around the veil that has recurred in a variety of forms in a number of Muslim and Arab countries since. As for those who took up Amin's call for unveiling in Egypt (such as Huda Sha'rawi), an upper-class or upper-middle-class

background, and to some degree or other a Western cultural affiliation, have been typical of those who became advocates of unveiling. In Turkey, for example, Ataturk, who introduced westernizing reforms, including laws affecting women, repeatedly denounced the veil in terms that, like Amin's, reproduced the Western narrative and show that his concern was with how the custom reflected on Turkish men, allowing them to appear "uncivilized" and objects of "ridicule." In one speech Ataturk declared: "In some places I have seen women who put a piece of cloth or a towel or something like that over their heads to hide their faces, and who turn their backs or huddle themselves on the ground when a man passes by. What are the meaning and sense of this behaviour? Gentlemen, can the mothers and daughters of a civilized nation adopt this strange manner, this barbarous posture? It is a spectacle that makes the nation an object of ridicule. It must be remedied at once."[13]

Similarly, in the 1920s [sic] the Iranian ruler Reza Shah, also an active reformer and westernizer, went so far as to issue a proclamation banning the veil, a move which had the support of some upper-class women as well as upper-class men. The ban, which symbolized the Westerly direction in which the ruling class intended to lead the society and signaled the eagerness of the upper classes to show themselves to be "civilized," was quite differently received by the popular classes. Even rumors of the move provoked unrest; demonstrations broke out but were ruthlessly crushed. For most Iranians, women as well as men, the veil was not, as a historian of Iranian women has observed, a "symbol of backwardness," which members of the upper classes maintained it was, but "a sign of propriety and a means of protection against the menacing eyes of male strangers." The police had instructions to deal harshly with any woman wearing anything other than a European-style hat or no headgear at all, and many women chose to stay at home rather than venture outdoors and risk having their veils pulled off by the police.[14]

In their stinging contempt for the veil and the savagery with which they attack it, these two members of the ruling class, like Amin, reveal their true motivations: they are men of the classes assimilating to European ways and smarting under the humiliation of being described as uncivilized because "their" women are veiled, and they are determined to eradicate the practice. That is to say, theirs are the words and acts of men exposed to the Western discourse who have accepted its representation of their culture, the inferiority of its practices, and the meaning of the veil. Why Muslim men should be making such statements and enacting such bans is only intelligible against the background of the global dominance of the Western world and the authority of its discourses, and also against the background of the ambiguous position of men and women of the upper classes, members of Muslim societies whose economic interests and cultural aspirations bound them to the colonizing West and who saw their own society partly through Western eyes.

The origins and history, just described, of the idea of the veil as it informs Western colonial discourse *and* twentieth-century Arabic debate have a number of implications. First, it is evident that the connection between the issues of culture and women, and more precisely between the cultures of Other men and the oppression of women, was created by Western discourse. The idea (which still often informs discussions about women in Arab and Muslim cultures and other non-Western world cultures) that improving the status of women entails abandoning native customs was the product of a particular historical moment and was constructed by an androcentric colonial establishment committed to male dominance in the service of particular political ends. Its absurdity and essential falseness become particularly apparent (at least from a feminist point of view) when one bears

Gillo Pontecorvo, *The Battle of Algiers*, 1965. Film still, 35mm, 120 mins. Reproduced by kind permission of Zaphira Yacef.

Faisal Abdu'Allah, *The Last
Supper*, 1995. Computer-
generated bromide prints
with selenium split tone on
photographic paper, mounted
on aluminium, 136 x 191cm.
Arts Council Collection, England.

in mind that those who first advocated it believed that Victorian mores and dress, and Victorian Christianity, represented the ideal to which Muslim women should aspire.

Second, these historical origins explain another and, on the face of it, somewhat surprising phenomenon: namely, the peculiar resemblance to be found between the colonial and still-commonplace Western view that an innate connection exists between the issues of culture and women in Muslim societies and the similar presumption underlying the Islamic resistance position, that such a fundamental connection does indeed exist. The resemblance between the two positions is not coincidental: they are mirror images of each other. The resistance narrative contested the colonial thesis by inverting it – thereby also, ironically, grounding itself in the premises of the colonial thesis.

The preceding account of the development of a colonial narrative of women in Islam has other implications as well, including that the colonial account of Islamic oppression of women was based on misperceptions and political manipulations and was incorrect. My argument here is not that Islamic societies did not oppress women. They did and do; that is not in dispute. Rather, I am here pointing to the political uses of the idea that Islam oppressed women and noting that what patriarchal colonialists identified as the sources and main forms of women's oppression in Islamic societies was based on a vague and inaccurate understanding of Muslim societies. This means, too, that the feminist agenda for Muslim women as set by Europeans – and first devised by the likes of Cromer – was incorrect and irrelevant. It was incorrect in its broad assumptions that Muslim women needed to abandon native ways and adopt those of the West to improve their status; obviously, Arab and Muslim women need to reject (just as Western women have been trying to do) the androcentrism and misogyny of whatever culture and tradition they find themselves in, but that is not at all the same as saying they have to adopt Western culture or reject Arab culture and Islam comprehensively. The feminist agenda as defined by Europeans was also incorrect in its particularities, including its focus on the veil. Because of this history of struggle around it, the veil is now pregnant with meanings. As an item of clothing, however, the veil itself and whether it is worn are about as relevant to substantive matters of women's rights as the social prescription of one or another item of clothing is to Western women's struggles over substantive issues. When items of clothing – be it bloomers or bras – have briefly figured as focuses of contention and symbols of feminist struggle in Western societies, it was at least Western feminist women who were responsible for identifying the item in question as significant and defining it as a site of struggle and not, as has sadly been the case with respect to the veil for Muslim women, colonial and patriarchal men, like Cromer and Amin, who declared it important to feminist struggle.

That so much energy has been expended by Muslim men and then Muslim women to remove the veil and by others to affirm or restore it is frustrating and ludicrous. But even worse is the legacy of meanings and struggles over issues of culture and class with which not only the veil but also the struggle for women's rights as a whole has become inscribed as a result of this history and as a result of the cooptation by colonialism of the issue of women and the language of feminism in its attempt to undermine other cultures.

This history, and the struggles over culture and between classes, continues to live even today in the debates on the veil and on women. To a considerable extent, overtly or covertly, inadvertently or otherwise, discussions of women in Islam in academies and outside them, and in Muslim countries and outside them, continue either to reinscribe the Western narrative of Islam as oppressor and the West as liberator and native classist versions of that narrative or, conversely, to reinscribe the contentions of the Arabic narrative of resistance as to the essentialness of preserving Muslim customs, particularly with regard to women, as a sign of resistance to imperialism, whether colonial or postcolonial.[15]

Further, colonialism's use of feminism to promote the culture of the colonizers and undermine native culture has ever since imparted to feminism in non-Western societies the taint of having served as an instrument of colonial domination, rendering it suspect in Arab eyes and vulnerable to the charge of being an ally of colonial interests. That taint has undoubtedly hindered the feminist struggle within Muslim societies.

Extracts taken from 'Chapter 8: The Discourse of the Veil', in *Women and Gender in Islam*, New Haven and London: Yale University Press, 1992, pp. 144–68.

Notes

1. Earl of Cromer, *Modern Egypt*, 2 vols. (New York: Macmillan, 1908), 2:155; hereafter cited in the text.

2. A. B. De Guerville, *New Egypt* (London: William Heinemann, 1906), 154.

3. Cromer Papers, cited in Judith E. Tucker, *Women in Nineteenth-Century Egypt* (Cambridge: Cambridge University Press, 1985), 122.

4. Cromer was so prominent in the antisuffrage movement that it was sometimes called the Curzon-Cromer combine after Cromer and Lord Curzon, first marquis of Keddleston. See Constance Rover, *Women's Suffrage and Party Politics in Britain, 1866–1914* (London: Routledge and Kegan Paul; Toronto: University of Toronto Press, 1967), 171–73; see also Brian Harrison, *Separate Spheres: The Opposition to Women's Suffrage in Britain* (New York: Holmes and Meier Publishers, 1978).

5. Rev. Robert Bruce, in *Report of the Centenary Conference on Protestant Missions of the World Held in Exeter Hall, London* (*June 9–19th*), 2 vols., ed. James Johnston (New York: F. H. Revell, [1889]), 1:18–19; Annie van Sommer and Samuel M. Zwemer, eds., *Our Moslem Sister: A Cry of Need from Lands of Darkness Interpreted by Those Who Heard It* (New York: F. H. Revell, 1907), 27–28; van Sommer and Zwemer, eds., *Daylight in the Harem* (Edinburgh: Oliphant, Anderson and Ferrier, 1911), 149–50.

6. Qassim Amin, *Tahrir al-mar'a*, in *Al-a'mal al-kamila li Qassim Amin*, 2 vols., ed. Muhammad 'Amara (Beirut: Al-mu'assasa al-'arabiyya lil-dirasat wa'l-nashr, 1976), 2:71–72; hereafter cited in the text. All quotations from *Tahrir al-mar'a* are from vol. 2.

7. Perhaps passages such as the above were contributed by 'Abdu or by others – Sa'd Zaghloul or Lutfi al'Sayyid – who have also been mentioned as collaborating with Amin. See Afaf Lutfi al-Sayyid Marsot, *Egypt and Cromer* (London: John Murray, 1968), 187.

8. Mukhtar Tuhami, *Al-sahafa wa'l-fikr wa'l-thawra, thalath ma'ariq fikriyya* (Baghdad: Dar ma'mun lil-tiba'a, 1976), 28.

9. Among the more interesting pieces on the subject are Judith Gran, "Impact of the World Market on Egyptian Women," *Middle East Research and Information Report*, no. 58 (1977): 3–7; and Juan Ricardo Cole, "Feminism, Class, and Islam in Turn-of-the-Century Egypt," *International Journal of Middle East Studies 13*, no. 4 (1981): 394–407.

10. Tuhami, *Thalath ma'ariq fikriyya*, 42–45.

11. Tal'at Harb, *Tarbiyet al-mar'a wa'l-hijab*, 2nd ed. (Cairo: Matba'at al-manar, 1905), e.g., 18, 19, 25, 29.

12. Frantz Fanon, *A Dying Colonialism*, trans. Haakon Chevalier (New York: Grove Press, 1967), 65. A useful discussion of the interconnections between thesis and antithesis and the ways in which antithesis may become locked in meanings posed by the thesis may be found in Joan W. Scott, "Deconstructing Equality-versus-Difference: Or, the Uses of Poststructuralist Theory for Feminism," *Feminist Studies 14*, no. 1 (1988): 33–49.

13. Ataturk, speech at Kastamonu, 1925, quoted in Bernard Lewis, *The Emergence of Modern Turkey* (London: Oxford University Press, 1961), 165. For further discussions of Turkish articulations, see S. Mardin, *The Genesis of Young Ottoman Thought* (Princeton: Princeton University Press, 1962); and O. Ozankaya, "Reflections of Semsiddin Sami on Women in the Period before the Advent of Secularism," in *Family in Turkish Society*, ed. T. Erder (Ankara: Turkish Social Science Association, 1985).

14. Guity Nashat, "Women in Pre-Revolutionary Iran: A Historical Overview," in *Women and Revolution in Iran*, ed. Nashat (Boulder, Colo: Westview Press, 1982), 27.

15. One problem with rebuttals of the Islamicist [sic] argument voiced by women of Muslim background (and others) generally, but not exclusively, based in the West is the extent to which they reproduce the Western narrative and its iteration in native upper-class voice without taking account of the colonialist and classist assumptions in which it is mired. This silent and surely inadvertent reinscription of racist and classist assumptions is in rebuttals offered from a "Marxist" perspective as much as in rebuttals aligned with the Western liberal position. See, for example, Mai Ghoussoub, "Feminism – or the Eternal Masculine – in the Arab World," *New Left Review 161* (January-February 1987): 3–18; and Azar Tabari, "The Women's Movement in Iran: A Hopeful Prognosis," *Feminist Studies 12*, no. 2 (1986): 343–60. The topic of Orientalism and the study of Arab women is addressed with particular acumen in Rosemary Sayigh, "Roles and Functions of Arab Women: A Reappraisal of Orientalism and Arab Women," *Arab Studies Quarterly 3*, no. 3 (1981): 258–74.

Mapping the Illusive
Zineb Sedira

How do you represent the unrepresentable, unrepresentable due to over exposure or lack of exposure? How do you represent that which has been drained of meaning, misrepresented to the point of over saturation, yet under appreciated and neglected to the point of absurdity? Is it even futile to attempt such an endeavour... maybe, it is advisable, perhaps not.[1]

The dilemma of how to represent the unrepresentable – in this instance, the veil – has been in the forefront of my mind for many years. To this day, it raises numerous questions, often without answers. For me, the veil has never been a simple sign, but one which always elicited a multitude of readings, both visible and invisible. As an artist I have spent years exploring the physical and the mental veil, negotiating the social and cultural boundaries and contexts that inform such an investigation, and asking whether it is feasible to write and communicate productively about the subject.

At first sight, my artistic practice refers to the veil as a visual motif. But the veil is never purely a physical code, delineated and present; it is also a transparent and subtle mental code. My postcolonial geography has marked my practice and I tend to draw upon the veil worn by Algerian women, because of my own personal history and experience. Each Muslim state is culturally, politically, economically and socially different. Colonial histories and subjugation have varied according to the particular country, which has had a profound effect on the way Muslims differ from one another in how they are positioned in terms of gender, class, language and other forms of cultural and political identity.

As the autobiographical – particularly my matrilineal personal history – is a central aspect of my work and research, it is important to recognise the (dis)continuities of my own experience and to understand the multiple readings that I present as an artist. My identity has been formed by at least two seemingly contrasting and sometimes conflicting traditions. On the one hand, I grew up in the Paris of the 1960s and 1970s, partly educated by and socialising in the dominant secular and Catholic tradition of France. Yet, simultaneously, my family and immediate community were Arab Muslims. In addition, London has further shaped my identity and, for the last seventeen years, I have lived away from the North African community. The differences between England and France, particularly their contrasting attitudes to cultural difference, have also contributed significantly to my rethinking representation and identity.[2]

Whilst I never wore the veil, my work returns frequently both to the veil as a motif and to the less visible effects of veiling which I describe as 'veiling-the-mind', a concept which addresses the shifting worlds of external censorship and its internalised counterpart – self-censorship. We believe we understand the external culture which surrounds us. But do we? What influences the way we view the Other? In the West, do we recognise how and when self-censorship comes into play? How often do we choose not to notice – or not to read – our surroundings, because doing so would make us feel uncomfortable? What veils do we hide behind everyday? What differences are there between the physical veil in Muslim culture and the mental veil in Western culture? It soon becomes apparent that the mental veil is not about a forced Muslim enclosure but rather about an awareness of the cultural paradigms that inform our ideas around sexuality, gender and emotional space. Veiling-the-mind has become a metaphor of mine for the (mis)reading of cultural signs; to counteract the Western view of veiling, I try not to resort to the literal veil in my artistic practice. Instead I refer to veiling-the-mind in order to explore the multiple forms of veiling in both Western and Muslim

Mapping the Illusive
Zineb Sedira

Left: Shadafarin Ghadirian,
Qajar series, 1998.
Photograph, 16 x 24cm.

Overleaf: Zineb Sedira,
Silent Sight, 2000.
Video projection, 12 mins.
Courtesy of The Agency.

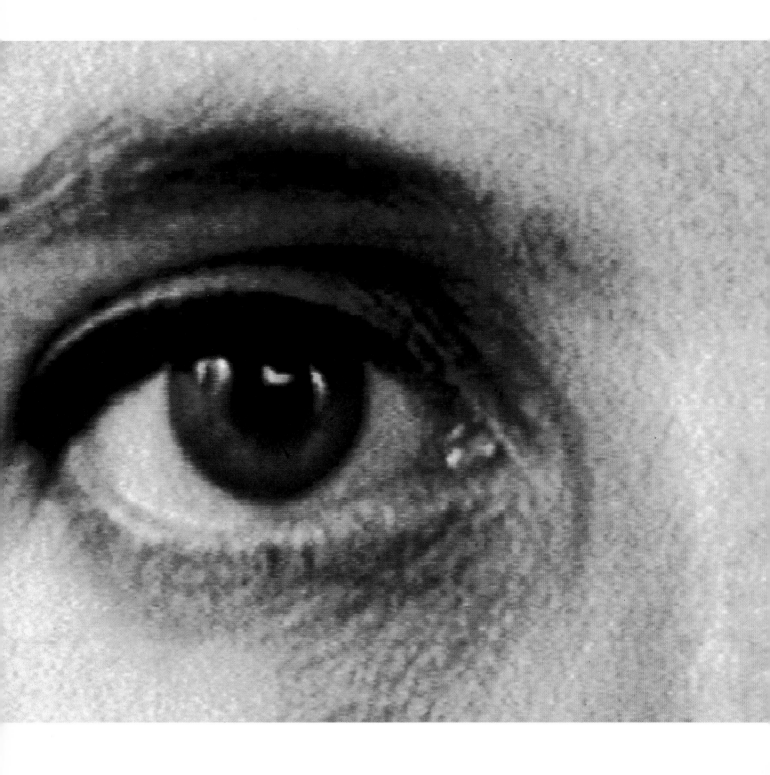

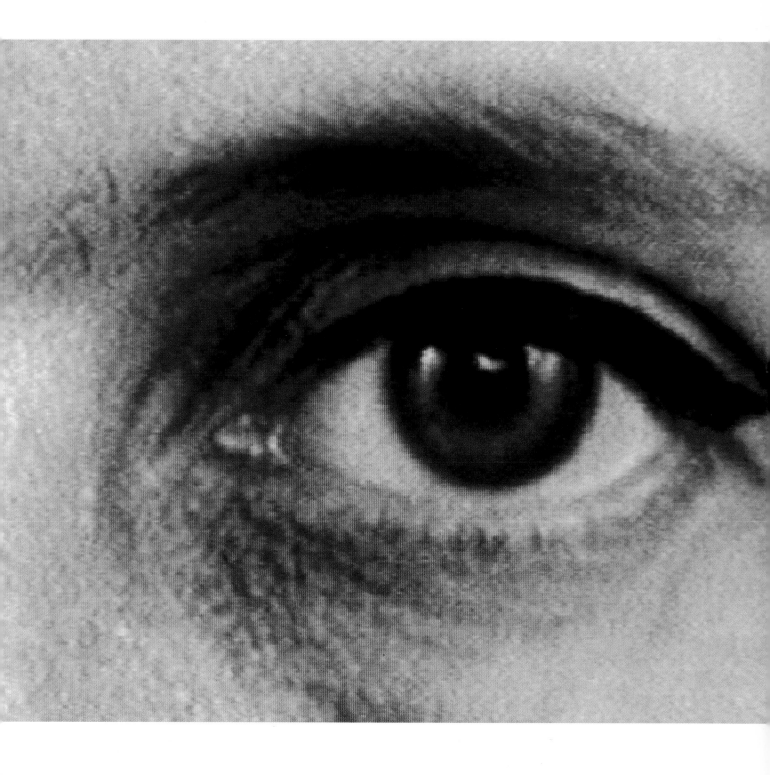

**Zineb Sedira, *Self-Portraits*
or *The Virgin Mary*, 2000.
Photographic triptych.
178 x 102cm. Courtesy of
The Agency.**

cultures. I find myself asking how to 'represent the unrepresentable' and my artistic interventions reveal my desire to open up the paradoxes, ambiguities and symbolism of the veil.

The idea of presenting a collection of writings and readings about the veil arose as I gathered together research, experience and observations around this complex symbol. The writings about – and readings of – the veil seemed, at first, to be confined to Western postcolonial or Orientalist debate. The apparent absence of the Muslim voice or experience created an unbalanced dialogue, a conversation with only one speaker. My subsequent research revealed what I had suspected – that a more complex and layered discourse around the veil was taking place amongst artists, writers and academics of Muslim origin – and this project evolved from the necessity of bringing these thoughts, works and studies into the Western frame. The gathering of dialogues evolved into a collaboration with other curators and artists and the work presented in the resulting exhibition is part of a continuing discussion on representation. The aim of the show was never to present a single reading of the veil, but to encourage concerns, questions and explorations to emerge.

How successfully an exhibition and publication can move that dialogue forward is a question that resonates throughout this essay. After all, how can I discuss the veil in Algeria without feeling the tensions of writing about constructed identities – such as 'Algeria' or 'the West' – which are socially produced and then used for political ends? How do I write about the subject of the veil in the West without worrying that my writing reinforces Orientalist fetishes, commodifying experience? Gayatri Spivak has expressed her reservations about postcolonial intellectuals who turn 'Third World' literature and experiences into 'commodities' to be consumed by the West. What space does this leave visual artists when exploring the veil as the object of representation? Can the artist escape the burden or cultural responsibility of representation? Is the artist, or indeed the curator, responsible for reinforcing the stereotypes of an audience? Mapping out an environment is not enough; instead, we must, as bell hooks suggests, transform the image – providing new strategies and readings – if we are to move the debate forward.

> [It] is not just a question of critiquing the status quo. It is also about transforming the image, creating alternatives, asking ourselves questions about what type of images subvert, pose critical alternatives, and transform our worldviews and move us away from dualistic thinking about good and bad. Making a space for the transgressive image, the outlaw rebel vision, is essential to any effort to create a context for transformation.[3]

The visual art in *Veil* has many readings, but I wish to foreground that of transgression. All the artists in this project communicate the personal and the collective, with photography, video, words, installations and sound as their media of expression and inscription. My ambition for such a dialogue was, and still remains, the need for a critique that enables a renewed lexicon with which to articulate the complexities and subtleties – the ambiguities and contradictions, the generalities and specificities, the similarities and differences – of veiling. Working creatively, sensitively and provocatively, such a lexicon could then speak to and about the paradoxes of the veil.

I am conscious about carrying the weight of translating cultural difference and, as a cross-cultural artist working in the West, I accept I can do little to disrupt this ever-present global cultural dominance. Do the interpretations and writings about artists' work instead serve to reinforce the limiting assumptions we are trying to subvert? I have

Elin Strand, *Speaking Bernina,* **2000. Video still, 16 mins.**

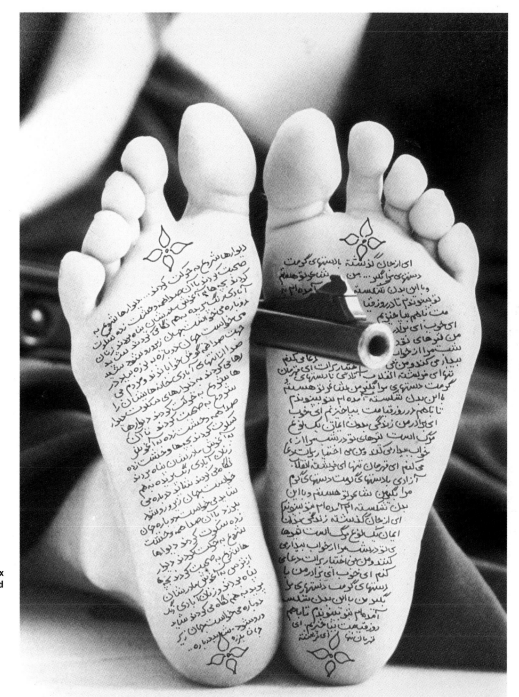

Shirin Neshat, *Allegiance with Wakefulness*, 1994. Black and white photograph with ink, 120 x 98.5cm. Collections of Eileen and Peter Norton, Santa Monica.

Ghada Amer, *Majnun* (detail),
1997. Embroidery on plastic
storage closets, 163 x 177cm.
Fonds National d'Art
Contemporain, Ministère de la
Culture et Communication, Paris
(FNAC: 971020) and Fonds
Régional d'Art Contemporain
Provence-Alpes-Côtes d'Azur.

Ghada Amer, *Black Series –*
Coulures Noires **(detail), 2000.**
Acrylic, embroidery and gel
medium on canvas, 173 x 178cm.

encountered critics and commentaries on the work of others and myself, where the reading of the work is limited and its richness and complexity lost. Carly Butler has raised this issue in reviewing Shirin Neshat's work. She notes that some interpretations of her work fit too comfortably with the existing ways we allow the Islamic world into our own, giving the viewer a sense of knowing control: 'The ambiguity disturbs us, yet through our transparent stereotypes we believe we must see bigger, less threatening issues such as global diaspora and displacement.'[4]

This inclination to read and communicate an understanding of the work without any cultural instruction is a study in itself, and would open up a series of very fruitful debates, since whenever we delve deeper, we find the deceptive simplicity unravels to reveal layers of visibility and invisibility.

Let us not pass too quickly over the tenacity of the veil. For the Western gaze, the veil and the Orient are so closely entwined. In his book *Orientalism*, Edward Said clearly states that for the West, the Orient 'was one of its deepest and most reoccurring images of the other'. He argues that one needs to examine Orientalism as a discourse in order to grasp that 'because of Orientalism the Orient was not (and is not) a free subject of thought or action'.[5] In our visually dominated culture, particular images of the veil have been deployed and replayed again and again to the point that it now seems almost impossible to represent the East, the Orient, or Islam without recourse to the veil. Repeatedly it has become a sign of the supposedly repressive Muslim world and implicit in that assumption is the superiority of the West in relation to that world. So transparent is this item of clothing to the Western gaze, that the veil has become an effective visual shorthand to signify

an extreme state of being – either repression or resistance. With such a long-established static visual language, how can I or any other visual artist bypass such representation?

The Muslim woman's body is central to Orientalist imagery as a voyeuristic site of Otherness and difference. The veil functions as a personal, cultural, religious and political emblem – an ideological object shrouded in fantasy and mystery. It has come to symbolise class, culture and the related conflict between colonised and coloniser – a site of contestation. The unveiled woman is seen as an individual and civilised subject, a far cry from the over-represented and culturally constructed veiled woman, who is considered anonymous, passive and exotic. The construction of gender in the Islamic world has already been mapped by the Western mind.

It is not the question of the body being under the veil, but that the identity and the body of the Arab Woman is made in the surface of her clothing, an interweaving of her skin and cloth; 'If the veil is part of her body, part of her being in the world, then it defers from a simple cover that has an inside and outside.... In the ambiguous position it occupies, the veil is not outside the woman's body. Nor is she the interior that needs to be protected or penetrated. Her body is not simply inside of the veil: it is of it; she is constituted in and by the fabrication of the veil.[6]

The physical veil has indeed become a spectacle. Not simply an item of clothing, it marks a cultural and emotional territory. Inscribed to the body, the distinction between the wearer and the cloth is made invisible; the Muslim woman's body – the medium through which power operates and functions – is defined by the surface of her clothing. This is a subtle but potent commentary on cultural experiences and

Preceding pages: Marc Garanger,
***Femmes Algériennes* (Algerian Women), 1960. Photographs, 30 x 40cm.**

codes, revealing the complexity of the gaze upon the Muslim woman.

The veil... has come to be one of the most visible and... debated external signs of difference, social positioning, gender, desire and exclusion/ inclusion. The veil is a complex symbol that carries a multiplicity of frequently shifting and often contradictory meanings in differing postcolonial geographies.[7]

There are, of course, no ready answers – nor should there be – to the questions and dilemmas that are part and parcel of the work in *Veil*. More important, however, is to continue asking questions – interrogating, deconstructing, reworking ideas about the veil – and to create a greater space to explore and understand veiling in all its multilayered, complex guises. The visual interventions within the exhibition attempt on a number of levels to disrupt this supposed unequivocal symbol. I am also concerned that *Veil* should not be seen as just another exhibition addressing postcolonial and diasporic issues, as the complexity and richness of the work is eclipsed by such a simplistic and limited reading. As Fadwa El Guindi asks, 'Veiling was and is a practice that is differentiated and variable, with each variant deeply embedded in the cultural system. Perhaps the whole issue should be reframed. Is it the same "veil" that is being documented throughout the millennia?'[8]

I would like to think that a reframing might include the investigation of the veil's role within contemporary Muslim society and the sacred meaning of the veil that connects it to cultural notions of sanctity and privacy. At this stage, however, I am not sure of the implication for contemporary artists, curators and writers of such a reframing. It merits further consideration.

Despite my questions and reservations, I have continued to want to work with themes relating to the veil and veiling. It is a real part of my history – personal and social, private and public. At a material level, veiling itself is a heterogeneous practice and the differences in veiling are reflected in the variety of work found in this exhibition. Visual artists, writers and curators need to continue to challenge the recurrent reductionism and work towards a critical, polyvocal dialogue. And *Veil*, I hope, will play a small part towards achieving this.

Images we have of each other are part of the baggage we bring to dialogue. Sometimes we are at the mercy of our image; sometimes we hide behind it; sometimes we act as though neither of us had an image of the other.... It is the degree to which image is present in dialogue that affects the ways in which identity is articulated.[9]

Notes

1. Salloum, Jayce. *Intangible Cartographies: New Arab Video*, exhibition catalogue, Worldwide Video Festival 2001.
2. Sedira, Zineb and Jawad Al-Nawab. 'On Becoming an Artist: Algerian, African, Arab, Muslim, French *and* Black British', in *Shades of Black*. London: inIVA, forthcoming.
3. hooks, bell. *Black Looks: Race and Representation*. Boston: South End Press, 1992.
4. Butler, Carly. 'Ambivalence and Iranian Identity: The Work of Shirin Neshat', in *Eastern Art Report*, 2001–2, no. 47, p. 46.
5. Said, Edward. *Orientalism*. New York: Pantheon Books, 1978.
6. Yegenoglu, Meyda. *Colonial Fantasies: Towards a Feminist Reading of Orientalism*. Cambridge: Cambridge University Press, 1998, pp. 118–19.
7. Lloyd, Fran. 'Arab Women Artists: Issues of Representation and Gender in Contemporary British Visual Culture', in *Journal of Visual Culture in Britain*, 2001, vol. 2. no. 2, pp. 1–15.
8. El Guindi, Fadwa. *Veil: Modesty, Privacy and Resistance*. New York and Oxford: Berg, 1999.
9. Cooke, Miriam. 'The Weight of the Veil', in *Women Claim ISLAM – Creating Islamic Feminism through Literature*. New York: Routledge, 2001, p. 130.

Algeria Unveiled
Frantz Fanon

It is by their apparel that types of society first become known, whether through written accounts and photographic records or motion pictures. Thus, there are civilizations without neckties, civilizations with loin-cloths, and others without hats. The fact of belonging to a given cultural group is usually revealed by clothing traditions. In the Arab world, for example, the veil worn by women is at once noticed by the tourist. One may remain for a long time unaware of the fact that a Moslem does not eat pork or that he denies himself daily sexual relations during the month of Ramadan, but the veil worn by the women appears with such constancy that it generally suffices to characterize Arab society.

In the Arab Maghreb, the veil belongs to the clothing traditions of the Tunisian, Algerian, Moroccan and Libyan national societies. For the tourist and the foreigner, the veil demarcates both Algerian society and its feminine component. In the case of the Algerian man, on the other hand, regional modifications can be noted: the *fez* in urban centers, turbans and *djellabas* in the countryside. The masculine garb allows a certain margin of choice, a modicum of heterogeneity. The woman seen in her white veil unifies the perception that one has of Algerian feminine society. Obviously what we have here is a uniform which tolerates no modification, no variant.

The *haïk* very clearly demarcates the Algerian colonized society. It is of course possible to remain hesitant before a little girl, but all uncertainty vanishes at the time of puberty. With the veil, things become well-defined and ordered. The Algerian woman, in the eyes of the observer, is unmistakably "she who hides behind a veil."

We shall see that this veil, one of the elements of the traditional Algerian garb, was to become the bone of contention in a grandiose battle, on account of which the occupation forces were to mobilize their most powerful and most varied resources, and in the course of which the colonized were to display a surprising force of inertia. Taken as a whole, colonial society, with its values, its areas of strength, and its philosophy, reacts to the veil in a rather homogeneous way. The decisive battle was launched before 1954, more precisely during the early 1930s. The officials of the French administration in Algeria, committed to bring about the disintegration, at whatever cost, of forms of existence likely to evoke a national reality directly or indirectly, were to concentrate their efforts on the wearing of the veil, which was looked upon at this juncture as a symbol of the status of the Algerian woman. Such a position is not the consequence of a chance intuition. It is on the basis of the analyses of sociologists and ethnologists that the specialists in so-called native affairs and the heads of the Arab Bureaus coordinated their work. At an initial stage, there was a pure and simple adoption of the well-known formula, "Let's win over the women and the rest will follow." This definition of policy merely gave a scientific coloration to the "discoveries" of the sociologists.

Beneath the patrilineal pattern of Algerian society, the specialists described a structure of matrilineal essence. Arab society has often been presented by Westerners as a formal society in which outside appearances are paramount. The Algerian woman, an intermediary between obscure forces and the group, appeared in this perspective to assume a primordial importance. Behind the visible, manifest patriarchy, the more significant existence of a basic matriarchy was affirmed. The role of the Algerian mother, that of the grandmother, the aunt and the "old woman," were inventoried and defined.

This enabled the colonial administration to define a precise political doctrine: "If we want to destroy the structure of Algerian society, its capacity for resistance, we must first of all conquer the women; we must go and find them behind the veil where they hide

Algeria Unveiled
Frantz Fanon

themselves and in the houses where the men keep them out of sight." It is the situation of woman that was accordingly taken as the theme of action. The dominant administration solemnly undertook to defend this woman, pictured as humiliated, sequestered, cloistered.... It described the immense possibilities of woman, unfortunately transformed by the Algerian man into an inert, demonetized, indeed dehumanized object. The behavior of the Algerian was very firmly denounced and described as medieval and barbaric. With infinite science, a blanket indictment against the "sadistic and vampirish" Algerian attitude toward women was prepared and drawn up. Around the family life of the Algerian, the occupier piled up a whole mass of judgments, appraisals, reasons, accumulated anecdotes and edifying examples, thus attempting to confine the Algerian within a circle of guilt.

Mutual aid societies and societies to promote solidarity with Algerian women sprang up in great number. Lamentations were organized. "We want to make the Algerian ashamed of the fate that he metes out to women." This was a period of effervescence, of putting into application a whole technique of infiltration, in the course of which droves of social workers and women directing charitable works descended on the Arab quarters.

The indigent and famished women were the first to be besieged. Every kilo of semolina distributed was accompanied by a dose of indignation against the veil and the cloister. The indignation was followed up by practical advice. Algerian women were invited to play "a functional, capital role" in the transformation of their lot. They were pressed to say no to a centuries-old subjection. The immense role they were called upon to play was described to them. The colonial administration invested great sums in this combat. After it had been posited that the woman constituted the pivot of Algerian society, all efforts were made to obtain control over her. The Algerian, it was assured, would not stir, would resist the task of cultural destruction undertaken by the occupier, would oppose assimilation, so long as his woman had not reversed the stream. In the colonialist program, it was the woman who was given the historic mission of shaking up the Algerian man. Converting the woman, winning her over to the foreign values, wrenching her free from her status, was at the same time achieving a real power over the man and attaining a practical, effective means of destructuring Algerian culture.

Still today, in 1959, the dream of a total domestication of Algerian society by means of "unveiled women aiding and sheltering the occupier" continues to haunt the colonial authorities.

The Algerian men, for their part, are a target of criticism for their European comrades, or more officially for their bosses. There is not a European worker who does not sooner or later, in the give and take of relations on the job site, the shop or the office, ask the Algerian the ritual questions: "Does your wife wear the veil? Why don't you take your wife to the movies, to the fights, to the café?"

European bosses do not limit themselves to the disingenuous query or the glancing invitation. They use "Indian cunning" to corner the Algerian and push him to painful decisions. In connection with a holiday – Christmas or New Year, or simply a social occasion with the firm – the boss will invite *the Algerian employee and his wife*. The invitation is not a collective one. Every Algerian is called in to the director's office and invited by name to come with "your little family." "The firm being one big family, it would be unseemly for some to come without their wives, you understand?..." Before this formal summons, the Algerian sometimes experiences moments of difficulty. If he comes with his wife, it means admitting defeat, it means "prostituting his wife," exhibiting her, abandoning a mode of resistance. On the other hand, going alone means refusing to give satisfaction to the boss; it means running the risk of being out of a job. The study of a case chosen at random – a description of the traps set by the Europeans in order to bring the Algerian to expose himself, to declare: "My wife wears a veil, she shall not go out," or else to betray: "Since you want to see her, here she is," – would bring out the sadistic and perverse character of these contacts and relationships and would show in microcosm the tragedy of the colonial situation on the psychological level, the way the two systems directly confront each other, the epic of the colonized society, with its specific ways of existing, in the face of the colonialist hydra....

The phenomena of counter-acculturation must be understood as the organic impossibility of a culture to modify any one of its customs without at the same time re-evaluating its deepest values, its most stable models. To speak of counter-acculturation in a colonial situation is an absurdity. The phenomena of resistance observed in the colonized must be related to an attitude of counter-assimilation, of maintenance of a cultural, hence national, originality.

The occupying forces, in applying their maximum psychological attention to the veil worn by Algerian women, were obviously bound to achieve some results. Here and there it thus happened that a woman was "saved," and symbolically unveiled.

These test-women, with bare faces and free bodies, henceforth circulated like sound currency in the European society of Algeria. These women were surrounded by an atmosphere of newness. The Europeans, over-excited and wholly given over to their victory, carried away in a kind of trance, would speak of the psychological phenomena of conversion. And in fact, in the European society, the agents of this conversion were held in esteem. They were envied. The benevolent attention of the administration was drawn to them.

After each success, the authorities were strengthened in their conviction that the Algerian woman would support Western penetration into the native society. Every rejected veil disclosed to the eyes of the colonialists horizons until then forbidden, and revealed to them, piece by piece, the flesh of Algeria laid bare. The occupier's aggressiveness, and hence his hopes, multiplied ten-fold each time a new face was uncovered. Every new Algerian woman unveiled announced to the occupier an Algerian society whose systems of defense were in the process of dislocation, open and breached. Every veil that fell, every body that became liberated from the traditional embrace of the *haïk*, every face that offered itself to the bold and impatient glance of the occupier, was a negative expression of the fact that Algeria was beginning to deny herself and was accepting the rape of the colonizer. Algerian society with every abandoned veil seemed to express its willingness to attend the master's school and to decide to change its habits under the occupier's direction and patronage.

We have seen how colonial society, the colonial administration, perceives the veil, and we have sketched the dynamics of the efforts undertaken to fight it as an institution and the resistances developed by the colonized society. At the level of the individual, of the private European, it may be interesting to follow the multiple reactions provoked by the existence of the veil, which reveal the original way in which the Algerian woman manages to be present or absent.

For a European not directly involved in this work of conversion, what reactions are there to be recorded?

The dominant attitude appears to us to be a romantic exoticism, strongly tinged with sensuality.

And, to begin with, the veil hides a beauty.

A revealing reflection – among others – of this state of mind was communicated to us by a European visiting Algeria who, in the exercise of his profession (he was a lawyer), had had the opportunity of seeing a few Algerian women without the veil. These men, he said, speaking of the Algerians, are guilty of concealing so many strange beauties. It was his conclusion that a people with a cache of such prizes, of such perfections of nature, owes it to itself to show them, to exhibit them. If worst came to worst, he added, it ought to be possible to force them to do so....

But there is also in the European the crystallization of an aggressiveness, the strain of a kind of violence before the Algerian woman. Unveiling this woman is revealing her beauty; it is baring her secret, breaking her resistance, making her available for adventure. Hiding the face is also disguising a secret; it is also creating a world of mystery, of the hidden. In a confused way, the European experiences his relation with the Algerian woman at a highly complex level. There is in it the will to bring this woman within his reach, to make her a possible object of possession.

This woman who sees without being seen frustrates the colonizer. There is no reciprocity. She does not yield herself, does not give herself, does not offer herself.... The European faced with an Algerian woman wants to see. He reacts in an aggressive way before this limitation of his perception. Frustration and aggressiveness, here too, evolve apace....

In a medical consultation, for example, at the end of the morning, it is common to hear European doctors express their disappointment. The women who remove their veils before them are commonplace, vulgar; there is really nothing to make such a mystery of. One wonders what they are hiding.

European women settle the conflict in a much less round-about way. They blatantly affirm that no one hides what is beautiful and discern in this strange custom an "altogether feminine" intention of disguising imperfections. And they proceed to compare the strategy of the European woman, which is intended to correct, to embellish, to bring out (beauty treatments, hairdos, fashion), with that of the Algerian woman, who prefers to veil, to conceal, to cultivate the man's doubt and desire. On another level, it is claimed that

the intention is to mislead the customer, and that the wrapping in which the "merchandise" is presented does not really alter its nature, nor its value.

The content of the dreams of Europeans brings out other special themes. Jean-Paul Sartre, in his *Réflections Sur la Question Juive* [sic], has shown that on the level of the unconscious, the Jewish woman almost always has an aura of rape about her.

The history of the French conquest in Algeria, including the overrunning of villages by the troops, the confiscation of property and the raping of women, the pillaging of a country, has contributed to the birth and the crystallization of the same dynamic image. At the level of the psychological strata of the occupier, the evocation of this freedom given to the sadism of the conqueror, to his eroticism, creates faults, fertile gaps through which both dreamlike forms of behavior and, on certain occasions, criminal acts can emerge.

Thus the rape of the Algerian woman in the dream of a European is always preceded by a rending of the veil. We here witness a double deflowering. Likewise, the woman's conduct is never one of consent or acceptance, but of abject humility....

We have seen that on the level of individuals the colonial strategy of destructuring Algerian society very quickly came to assign a prominent place to the Algerian woman. The colonialist's relentlessness, his methods of struggle were bound to give rise to reactionary forms of behavior on the part of the colonized. In the face of the violence of the occupier, the colonized found himself defining a principled position with respect to a formerly inert element of the native cultural configuration. It was the colonialist's frenzy to unveil the Algerian woman, it was his gamble on winning the battle of the veil at whatever cost, that were to provoke the native's bristling resistance. The deliberately aggressive intentions of the colonialist with respect to the *haïk* gave a new life to this dead element of the Algerian cultural stock – dead because

stabilized, without any progressive change in form or color. We here recognize one of the laws of the psychology of colonization. In an initial phase, it is the action, the plans of the occupier that determine the centers of resistance around which a people's will to survive becomes organized.

It is the white man who creates the Negro. But it is the Negro who creates negritude. To the colonialist offensive against the veil, the colonized opposes the cult of the veil. What was an undifferentiated element in a homogeneous whole acquires a taboo character, and the attitude of a given Algerian woman with respect to the veil will be constantly related to her overall attitude with respect to the foreign occupation. The colonized, in the face of the emphasis given by the colonialist to this or that aspect of his traditions, reacts very violently....

Upon the outbreak of the struggle for liberation, the attitude of the Algerian woman, or of native society in general, with regard to the veil was to undergo important modifications. These innovations are of particular interest in view of the fact that they were at no time included in the program of the struggle. The doctrine of the Revolution, the strategy of combat, never postulated the necessity for a revision of forms of behavior with respect to the veil. We are able to affirm even now that when Algeria has gained her independence such questions will not be raised, for in the practice of the Revolution the people have understood that problems are resolved in the very movement that raises them....

During the whole period of unchallenged domination, we have seen that Algerian society, and particularly the women, had a tendency to flee from the occupier. The tenacity of the occupier in his endeavor to unveil the women, to make of them an ally in the work of cultural destruction, had the effect of strengthening the traditional patterns of behavior. These patterns, which were essentially positive in the strategy of

resistance to the corrosive action of the colonizer, naturally had negative effects. The woman, especially the city woman, suffered a loss of ease and of assurance. Having been accustomed to confinement, her body did not have the normal mobility before a limitless horizon of avenues, of unfolded sidewalks, of houses, of people dodged or bumped into. This relatively cloistered life, with its known, categorized, regulated comings and goings, made any immediate revolution seem a dubious proposition....

The decision as to whether or not the women were to participate in the Revolution had to be made; the inner oppositions became massive, and each decision gave rise to the same hesitations, produced the same despair.

In the face of the extraordinary success of this new form of popular combat, observers have compared the action of the Algerian women to that of certain women resistance fighters or even secret agents of the specialized services....

The woman who might be acting as a liaison agent, as a bearer of tracts, as she walked some hundred or two hundred meters ahead of the man under whose orders she was working, still wore a veil; but after a certain period the pattern of activity that the struggle involved shifted in the direction of the European city. The protective mantle of the Kasbah, the almost organic curtain of safety that the Arab town weaves round the native, withdrew, and the Algerian woman, exposed, was sent forth into the conqueror's city....

An unveiled Algerian girl who "walks the street" is very often noticed by young men who behave like young men all over the world, but who use a special approach as the result of the idea people habitually have of one who has discarded the veil. She is treated to unpleasant, obscene, humiliating remarks. When such things happen, she must grit her teeth, walk away a few steps, elude the passers-by who draw attention to her, who give other passers-by the desire either to

Gillo Pontecorvo, *The Battle of Algiers*, 1965. Film still, 35mm, 120 mins. Reproduced by kind permission of Zaphira Yacef.

follow their example, or to come to her defense. Or it may be that the Algerian woman is carrying in her bag or in a small suitcase twenty, thirty, forty million francs, money belonging to the Revolution, money which is to be used to take care of the needs of the families of prisoners, or to buy medicine and supplies for the guerrillas.

This revolutionary activity has been carried on by the Algerian woman with exemplary constancy, self-mastery, and success. Despite the inherent, subjective difficulties and notwithstanding the sometimes violent incomprehension of a part of the family, the Algerian woman assumes all the tasks entrusted to her....

From this point on the Algerian woman became wholly and deliberately immersed in the revolutionary action. It was she who would carry in her bag the grenades and the revolvers that a *fidaï* would take from her at the last moment, before the bar, or as a designated criminal passed. During this period Algerians caught in the European city were pitilessly challenged, arrested, searched.

This is why we must watch the parallel progress of this man and this woman, of this couple that brings death to the enemy, life to the Revolution. The one supporting the other, but apparently strangers to each other. The one radically transformed into a European woman, poised and unconstrained, whom no one would suspect, completely at home in the environment, and the other, a stranger, tense, moving toward his destiny....

Carrying revolvers, grenades, hundreds of false identity cards or bombs, the unveiled Algerian woman moves like a fish in the Western waters. The soldiers, the French patrols, smile to her as she passes, compliments on her looks are heard here and there, but no one suspects that her suitcases contain the automatic pistol which will presently mow down four or five members of one of the patrols.

We must come back to that young girl, unveiled only yesterday, who walks with sure steps down the street of the European city teeming with policemen, parachutists, militiamen. She no longer slinks along the walls as she tended to do before the Revolution. Constantly called upon to efface herself before a member of the dominant society, the Algerian woman avoided the middle of the sidewalk which in all countries in the world belongs rightfully to those who command.

The shoulders of the unveiled Algerian woman are thrust back with easy freedom. She walks with a graceful, measured stride, neither too fast nor too slow. Her legs are bare, not confined by the veil, given back to themselves, and her hips are free.

The body of the young Algerian woman, in traditional society, is revealed to her by its coming to maturity and by the veil. The veil covers the body and disciplines it, tempers it, at the very time when it experiences its phase of greatest effervescence. The veil protects, reassures, isolates. One must have heard the confessions of Algerian women or have analyzed the dream content of certain recently unveiled women to appreciate the importance of the veil for the body of the woman. Without the veil she has an impression of her body being cut up into bits, put adrift; the limbs seem to lengthen indefinitely. When the Algerian woman has to cross a street, for a long time she commits errors of judgment as to the exact distance to be negotiated. The unveiled body seems to escape, to dissolve. She has an impression of being improperly dressed, even of being naked. She experiences a sense of incompleteness with great intensity. She has the anxious feeling that something is unfinished, and along with this a frightful sensation of disintegrating. The absence of the veil distorts the Algerian woman's corporal pattern. She quickly has to invent new dimensions for her body, new means of muscular control. She has to create for herself an attitude of

Gillo Pontecorvo, *The Battle of Algiers*, 1965. Film still, 35mm, 120 mins. Reproduced by kind permission of Zaphira Yacef.

unveiled-woman-outside. She must overcome all timidity, all awkwardness (for she must pass for a European), and at the same time be careful not to overdo it, not to attract notice to herself. The Algerian woman who walks stark naked into the European city relearns her body, re-establishes it in a totally revolutionary fashion. This new dialectic of the body and of the world is primary in the case of one revolutionary woman.

But the Algerian woman is not only in conflict with her body. She is a link, sometimes an essential one, in the revolutionary machine. She carries weapons, knows important points of refuge. And it is in terms of the concrete dangers that she faces that we must gauge the insurmountable victories that she has had to win in order to be able to say to her chief, on her return: "Mission accomplished... R.A.S."

Another difficulty to which attention deserves to be called appeared during the first months of feminine activity. In the course of her comings and goings, it would happen that the unveiled Algerian woman was seen by a relative or a friend of the family. The father was sooner or later informed. He would naturally hesitate to believe such allegations. Then more reports would reach him. Different persons would claim to have seen "Zohra or Fatima unveiled, walking like a... My Lord, protect us!..." The father would then decide to demand explanations. He would hardly have begun to speak when he would stop. From the young girl's look of firmness the father would have understood that her commitment was of long standing. The old fear of dishonor was swept away by a new fear, fresh and cold – that of death in battle or of torture of the girl. Behind the girl, the whole family – even the Algerian father, the authority for all things, the founder of every value – following in her footsteps, becomes committed to the new Algeria.

Removed and reassumed again and again, the veil has been manipulated, transformed into a technique of camouflage, into a means of struggle. The virtually taboo character assumed by the veil in the colonial situation disappeared almost entirely in the course of the liberating struggle. Even Algerian women not actively integrated into the struggle formed the habit of abandoning the veil. It is true that under certain conditions, especially from 1957 on, the veil reappeared. The missions in fact became increasingly difficult. The adversary now knew, since certain militant women had spoken under torture, that a number of women very Europeanized in appearance were playing a fundamental role in the battle. Moreover, certain European women of Algeria were arrested, to the consternation of the adversary who discovered that his own system was breaking down. The discovery by the French authorities of the participation of Europeans in the liberation struggle marks a turning point in the Algerian Revolution. From that day, the French patrols challenged every person. Europeans and Algerians were equally suspect. All historic limits crumbled and disappeared. Any person carrying a package could be required to open it and show its contents. Anyone was entitled to question anyone as to the nature of a parcel carried in Algiers, Philippeville, or Batna. Under those conditions it became urgent to conceal the package from the eyes of the occupier and again to cover oneself with the protective *haïk*.

Here again, a new technique had to be learned: how to carry a rather heavy object dangerous to handle under the veil and still give the impression of having one's hands free, that there was nothing under this *haïk*, except a poor woman or an insignificant young girl. It was not enough to be veiled. One had to look so much like a "fatma" that the soldier would be convinced that this woman was quite harmless.

Very difficult. Three meters ahead of you the police challenge a veiled woman who does not look particularly suspect. From the anguished expression of the unit leader you have guessed that she is carrying

Gillo Pontecorvo, *The Battle of Algiers*, 1965. Film still, 35mm, 120 mins. Reproduced by kind permission of Zaphira Yacef.

a bomb, or a sack of grenades, bound to her body by a whole system of strings and straps. For the hands must be free, exhibited bare, humbly and abjectly presented to the soldiers so that they will look no further. Showing empty and apparently mobile and free hands is the sign that disarms the enemy soldier.

The Algerian woman's body, which in an initial phase was pared down, now swelled. Whereas in the previous period the body had to be made slim and disciplined to make it attractive and seductive, it now had to be squashed, made shapeless and even ridiculous. This, as we have seen, is the phase during which she undertook to carry bombs, grenades, machine-gun clips.

The enemy, however, was alerted, and in the streets one witnessed what became a commonplace spectacle of Algerian women glued to the wall, on whose bodies the famous magnetic detectors, the "frying pans," would be passed. Every veiled woman, every Algerian woman became suspect. There was no discrimination. This was the period during which men, women, children, the whole Algerian people, experienced at one and the same time their national vocation and the recasting of the new Algerian society.

Ignorant or feigning to be ignorant of these new forms of conduct, French colonialism, on the occasion of May 13th, reenacted its old campaign of Westernizing the Algerian woman. Servants under the threat of being fired, poor women dragged from their homes, prostitutes, were brought to the public square and *symbolically* unveiled to the cries of "*Vive l'Algérie française!*" Before this new offensive old reactions reappeared. Spontaneously and without being told, the Algerian women who had long since dropped the veil once again donned the *haïk*, thus affirming that it was not true that woman liberated herself at the invitation of France and of General de Gaulle.

Behind these psychological reactions, beneath this immediate and almost unanimous response, we again see the overall attitude of rejection of the values of the occupier, even if these values objectively be worth choosing. It is because they fail to grasp this intellectual reality, this characteristic feature (the famous sensitivity of the colonized), that the colonizers rage at always "doing them good in spite of themselves." Colonialism wants everything to come from it. But the dominant psychological feature of the colonized is to withdraw before any invitation of the conqueror's. In organizing the famous cavalcade of May 13th, colonialism has obliged Algerian society to go back to methods of struggle already outmoded. In a certain sense, the different ceremonies have caused a turning back, a regression....

After the 13th of May, the veil was resumed, but stripped once and for all of its exclusively traditional dimension.

There is thus a historic dynamism of the veil that is very concretely perceptible in the development of colonization in Algeria. In the beginning, the veil was a mechanism of resistance, but its value for the social group remained very strong. The veil was worn because tradition demanded a rigid separation of the sexes, but also because the occupier *was bent on unveiling Algeria*. In a second phase, the mutation occurred in connection with the Revolution and under special circumstances. The veil was abandoned in the course of revolutionary action. What had been used to block the psychological or political offensives of the occupier became a means, an instrument. The veil helped the Algerian woman to meet the new problems created by the struggle.

The colonialists are incapable of grasping the motivations of the colonized. It is the necessities of combat that give rise in Algerian society to new attitudes, to new modes of action, to new ways.

Extracts from 'Chapter 1: Algeria Unveiled', in *Studies in a Dying Colonialism*, rev. ed., London: Earthscan Publications (www.earthscan.co.uk), 1989, pp. 35–67. Originally published in French as *L'An Cinq de la Révolution Algérienne* in 1959 and first translated into English by Haakon Chevalier (New York: Monthly Review Press, 1965).

Marc Garanger, *Femme Algérienne* **(Algerian Woman), 1960. Photograph, 30 x 40cm.**

Foreword to *Marc Garanger:*
Femmes Algériennes 1960 (Paris:
Contrejour, 1982)

En 1960, je faisais mon service militaire en Algérie.

L'armée française avait décidé que les autochtones devaient avoir une carte d'identité française pour mieux contrôler leurs déplacements dans les "villages de regroupement".

Comme il n'y avait pas de photographe civil, on me demanda de photographier tous les gens des villages avoisinants : Aïn Terzine, Bordj Okhriss, le Merdour, le Meghnine, Souk el Khrémis.

J'ai ainsi photographié près de 2000 personnes, en grande majorité des femmes, à la cadence de 200 par jour.

Dans chaque village, les populations étaient convoquées par le chef de poste. C'est le visage des femmes qui m'a beaucoup impressionné. Elles n'avaient pas le choix. Elles étaient dans l'obligation de se dévoiler et de se laisser photographier. Elles devaient s'asseoir sur un tabouret, en plein air, devant le mur blanc d'une mechta.

J'ai reçu leur regard a bout portant, premier témoin de leur protestation muette, violente. Je veux leur rendre témoignage.

marc garanger

In 1960, I was doing my military service
in Algeria.

When the French arrived, they decided that
the natives should carry a French identity card,
so that it would be easier to control their
movements between the 'reassembled villages'.

As there was no civilian photographer, they asked
me to photograph everybody in the neighbouring
villages: Aïn Terzine, Bordj Okhriss, le Mezdour,
le Meglinine, Souk el Khrémis.

As a result, I photographed nearly two thousand
people, mainly women, at a rate of two hundred
a day.

In each village, the postmaster would call up the
residents. It was the faces of the women that
struck me most. They had no choice. They were
forced to unveil and be photographed. They had
to sit on a stool, outdoors, in front of the white
wall of a house.

They glared at me from point-blank range; I was
the first to witness their silent but fierce protest.

In return, I want my photographs to bear witness
to them.

Marc Garanger, March 1982

Acting Out
Jananne Al-Ani

Debate around the veil is one of the remaining subjects which persistently invokes the tired and clichéd binaries of East/West, black/white, male/female. By retracing the well-trodden route of examining the representation of the veil from a feminist perspective, or in a colonial and post-colonial context, this essay examines how the activity of reworking a particular authority in relation to representation can help us to see historic works with new eyes.

In order to begin to unravel the amazing legacy of photographic material which has survived from the nineteenth and early twentieth centuries and which acts as a springboard for a number of artists in this exhibition, it is necessary to go back, yet again, over the history of European imperialism in the Middle East and North Africa and to examine the colonial project in light of the development of the related sciences of photography, anthropology and archaeology. By the late nineteenth century, European photographers were wanting primarily to document the biblical landscape and, secondarily, to focus on the locals, particularly the women. Implicit within these two distinct traditions, and as a result of the technical requirements of the medium, was the need for formal posing and staging. The set or backdrop for these early photographs was the photographic studio or the landscape of the desert and the performers, where required, were more often than not the natives. The relationship between the photographer, the stage and the actors is the thread that links together the works examined in this essay.

The prominent role of digital technology in the 1991 Desert Storm campaign was a watershed in the history of warfare and changed the way war was to be seen in the future. Within hours of the Iraqi invasion of Kuwait, the Western media machine had mobilised its forces and set its sights firmly on the region. Through the portrayal of the population, the culture and, crucially, the landscape of the Middle East, it revealed that the nineteenth-century Orientalist stereotype of the Arab and the desert remained firmly embedded in Western consciousness. The site of the war was shown to be a desert, a place with no history and no population – an empty space, a blank canvas.

In her essay *The Infinitive Image*,[1] Mounira Khemir writes about the desert and its representation in nineteenth-century European photography. She points out that, in English, 'to desert' is to leave a place empty whereas, in Arabic, the word *as-hara* (derived from the same root as the word for desert) means to have travelled into the desert, to have occupied it. This etymological distinction is an elegant illustration of the European vision of the desert as a blank screen on to which all manner of fantasies and desires could be projected. Khemir cites the coincidence of the invention of photography and the nineteenth-century interest in Egyptology and archaeology as the starting point for a relationship between the Western fantasy of the desert and its subsequent depiction by photographers, artists and writers. The major colonial expansion of the second half of the nineteenth century and the early twentieth century brought Europeans into contact with cultural difference on an unprecedented scale. Intrinsic to this consolidation by European powers was the desire to create an archive of all topics of contemporary life and history of a particular area and to make it completely open to scrutiny.

With an increasing dominance of ideas that valued technological and scientific achievement, photography represented the use of technological expertise to control the physical world; by photographing it, the world became knowable. By documenting and classifying the populations of colonised lands, anthropology and photography together transformed the power of knowing into a rationalised, observable truth.

The tale of the photographer Maxime du Camp – who visited Egypt and Palestine in 1848 and 1849 with the novelist Gustave Flaubert – exemplifies the

Above: *Caravan Passing the Hawara Pyramid on the Edge of the Desert near Cotton Field Flooded with Water*, Egypt. Stereoscopic photograph.

Below: *One of the Tombs of the Kings with the Stone Rolled Away*, Jerusalem, Palestine, 1903. Stereoscopic photograph.

Acting Out
Jananne Al-Ani

Caravan passing the Hawara Pyramid on edge of desert near cotton field flooded with water, Egypt.

(27) One of the "Tombs of the Kings," With the Stone Rolled away, Jerusalem, Palestine.
Copyright 1908 by Willard

Kourush Adim, *Le Voile*
(The Veil), 1999–2000.
Photographs, 50 x 60cm.

complex relationship between photography and power and the impulse of the photographer to 'stage' his work. Du Camp used Hajji Ismail, one of the sailors on the Nile steamer which the party was travelling on, to pose for him. 'In this way', he remarked, 'I was able to include a uniform scale of proportions on every one of my plates.' To persuade the man to remain still for the required length of time, he turned the camera into a weapon: 'I told him that the brass tube of the lens jutting out from the camera was a cannon, which would vomit a hail of shot if he had the misfortune to move – a story which immobilised him completely.'[2]

In the late 1830s, some of the earliest images of 'the Middle Eastern desert' were produced by photographers and artists who were attracted to the region as a site of pharaonic, classical and biblical antiquity. Throughout cities in the Middle East, European photographers established studios which produced thousands of photographs as postcards, stereoscopic slides, lantern slides and loose prints, primarily destined for the burgeoning tourist industry. The photographic studio was used as a theatrical set in which to present images of unnamed people whose only identity appeared in the often erroneous captions which categorised them by racial type, religion, tribe or, occasionally, class.

Photographs of Middle Eastern women drew heavily on a pre-existing repertoire of themes already established by the genre of Orientalist painting, among them, the harem, the odalisque, the white mistress and her black slave – images ranging from the ethnographic to the pornographic. In her exhaustive book on the representation of women in photography in the Middle East, *Images of Women*, Sarah Graham-Brown examines the relationship between the traditions of Orientalist painting and photography. For Graham-Brown, 'The difference between paintings and photographs... lies in the way they appear to the viewer. As Barthes suggests, this product of chemistry has a claim to "represent a reality" in a way no artist would claim for a painting. The process of photography, therefore, could transform these imaginative arrangements in the studio into "proof" of the way in which people in the Middle East and elsewhere looked and behaved.'[3]

The rather lowly position the Orientalist photographs occupy in the hierarchy of art objects is reflected in the photographic collections of museums and galleries in the West, such as the Bibliothèque Nationale in Paris and the Victoria and Albert Museum in London; the majority of photographs are considered mere curiosities with only the most technically and aesthetically accomplished prints being included. Amongst the few Orientalist photographs in the V&A's collection is an album of prints, *Femmes d'Orient*, published in Brussels in 1893. The photographs are accompanied by a short text in which the photographer La Comtesse de Croix-Mesnil favourably compares the position of women in Islam to that of Christian women, based on her experience of living in the East for five years. Despite its unusually positive spin on Islam, Croix-Mesnil's text is littered with clichés and stereotypes. She describes the Muslim woman as patient, loving and obedient, finding 'joy in the variety of distractions at the harem: the baths, the "nargileh"... patisserie, music, singing and dancing, the long siestas, visitors'. More interestingly, it is difficult to distinguish her photographs from the work of her male contemporaries who set up studios in the Middle East in the late nineteenth century. Indeed the curators of the collection now believe that the Comtesse herself may have been invented as a ruse to promote and sell the album to an expanding and increasingly curious Western market.[4]

By the end of the nineteenth century, there were a number of indigenous commercial photographic studios, many of which belonged to minority ethnic or religious groups, particularly the Armenians.[5]

Comtesse de Croix-Mesnil, *Portrait of a Mahometan Woman* from *Femmes d'Orient*, 1893. Photograph. © V&A Picture Library.

96 Veil

Although these studios produced much the same images – and stereotypes – for the tourist market as their European counterparts, a growing market for portrait photography emerged amongst the upper and middle classes. Imperial patronage also became common, particularly in Turkey and Iran. The best-known photographers of the era in Iran include Abdullah Qajar and Antoin Sevruguin, who became one of the official court photographers to Nasir al-din Shah (r. 1848–96).

The young Iranian photographer Shadafarin Ghadirian uses the court photographs of the Qajar dynasty as the starting point and inspiration for her own work. Ghadirian recreated a Qajar studio in her Tehran home, asking a painter friend to copy the backdrops. She made and borrowed period costumes and persuaded her friends and family to sit for her as she scrupulously choreographed the formal poses. She then added a can of Pepsi-Cola, a ghetto blaster, a vacuum cleaner and a mountain bike. Although she reproduces the studio of an indigenous photographer inspired by the European tradition, she allows us to witness the process of preparation, the work in progress, the painting of the backdrop and the selection of the costumes. As an artist working and exhibiting in Iran and also showing in the West, Ghadirian's work offers an example of how the signs and signifiers in her work are understood differently in different cultural contexts. For an Iranian audience, the contemporary props are seen as ordinary objects in an extraordinary costume drama, whereas for a Western audience – with no knowledge of the history of Iranian dress – the contemporary props disrupt what appears to be a timeless ethnographic portrait of an Other culture.

It is notable that Ghadirian chooses to focus on restaging portraits of the women of the Qajar court, a subject which forms only a small part of the indigenous archive of nineteenth-century photographs, but an inordinately large portion of the European

Comtesse de Croix-Mesnil, *Portrait of a Mahometan Woman* **from** *Femmes d'Orient*, **1893. Photograph.** © **V&A Picture Library.**

323   Intérieur mauresque — La danse

J. Geiser, phot.-Alger

Intérieur Mauresque – La Danse **(Moorish Interior – the Dance), late 19th–early 20th century. Postcard. Collection Michket Krifa.**

Shadafarin Ghadirian,
Qajar series, 1998.
Photographs, 16 x 24cm.

photographs produced in the Middle East. This can perhaps be explained by differing cultural attitudes towards the relationship between male photographers and their female subjects. In the Middle East, where the regulation of women's visibility was an important element of patriarchal control, photography not only asserted the photographer's power over the subject, but also suggested a loss of indigenous male control over 'their' women. Meanwhile, Western men's fantasies of what lay out of view were a common theme in the writings of the time.

> Sequestered within those inviolate walls are the two great mysteries of the East – its women and its wealth. Both are jealously guarded from the eye of the stranger; both are in the most literal sense of the word interred, for the manner of the Moor betrays nothing concerning the extent of the quality of his possessions.[6]

It is common throughout colonialist discourse for the figure of the woman to symbolise territory to be conquered, subdued and controlled. European images of Middle Eastern women express the relationship between West and East as that of master and slave, coloniser and colonised. The women depicted represent a passive, luxuriant Orient that is subservient to the West. The invisible yet controlling gaze of photographer and viewer was conceived in entirely masculine terms as both dominant and active. Approaching Egypt for the first time, Edward W. Lane confessed to feeling like a bridegroom 'about to lift the veil off his bride'.[7]

However, the majority of Westerners were shocked and affronted on first encountering veiled women in public, women who were visible yet invisible, seeing yet not seen. For Western men in particular, the veil presented a challenge, not only to the imagination, but to the right to scrutinise their subjects. In his book *The Colonial Harem*, Malek Alloula writes about the commercial photographs of Algerian women produced during the early twentieth century. For the photographer directing his camera at the veiled woman, the gaze he received in return could be disturbing and disarming.

> These veiled women are not only an embarrassing enigma to the photographer but an outright attack on him. It must be believed that the feminine gaze that filters through the veil is a gaze of a particular kind: concentrated by the tiny orifice for the eye, this womanly gaze is a little like the photographic lens that takes aim at everything.
>
> The photographer makes no mistake about it: he knows this gaze well; it resembles his own when it is extended by the dark chamber or the viewfinder. Thrust in the presence of a veiled woman, the photographer feels photographed; having himself become an object-to-be-seen, he loses initiative: *he is dispossessed of his own gaze.*[8]

One of the most significant bodies of work on the veil is that of the French psychiatrist Gaëtan de Clérambault. Clérambault was interested in mental automatism and passion-based psychoses. He produced two landmark texts on women's passion for fabrics. Clérambault enlisted as a medical officer during World War I and, after he was wounded, he was sent to Fez in Morocco to recuperate. It was only after his death that an archive of some four hundred photographs which he had taken of Moroccan women in the process of veiling were discovered.

Clérambault is a mysterious figure and little is known about the circumstances under which the images were made. What differentiates them from the Orientalist stereotyping, so dominant in the photography of his contemporaries, is the delicacy and sensitivity of

Gaëtan de Clérambault, *Morocco*, 1918–34. Photograph, 10 x 15cm. Collection Musée de l'Homme, Paris.

Gillo Pontecorvo, *The Battle of Algiers*, 1965. Film still, 35mm, 120 mins. Reproduced by kind permission of Zaphira Yacef.

the works. Many of the women are photographed in genuine interiors, unlike the stage sets of the commercial photographic studio; others are photographed outdoors, appearing active in the landscape. What interested Clérambault was the act of veiling itself and, in contrast to the dominant imagery of women becoming increasingly revealed to the extreme of nakedness, the women Clérambault photographs become increasingly hidden by the veil, while maintaining a strange and intimate relationship with the camera.

The veil, as a symbol, is not static but constantly shifting, according to differing historical and political contexts. For example, the removal of the veil in public in Egypt in the early part of the twentieth century was a sign of defiance and feminist resistance. By contrast, in Algeria in the 1950s and 1960s, the veil came to be seen by many, including the black intellectual and political activist Frantz Fanon, as a symbol of Arab resistance to French colonial oppression.

Working as a military photographer during the Algerian War of Independence (1954–62), Marc Garanger was ordered to unveil Algerian women forcibly in order to photograph them so that identity cards could be made. Garanger described the attitude of his superiors towards the photographs as an obscene, physical attack. In his view, it was as if the women had been raped twice; the first time was being forced to unveil and the second was having their photograph taken.

Resistance and confrontation is visible in the faces of the women Garanger photographed and many of them stare back at him with utter contempt. However, in some of the photographs, the women look submissive or uncomfortable, ambivalent even. Surprisingly, in yet others, they look relaxed and some even smile back at the camera. Although Garanger's portraits could be described as a perfect illustration of the relationship, through photography, between the coloniser and the colonised, the ambiguity that arises in a number of the portraits undermines this thesis. Is it possible for the compassion of the individual photographer to affect the outcome of an image in circumstances of such an extreme imbalance of power? Having been coerced himself into taking the photographs, is it possible that Garanger's sympathy for these women somehow affected the outcome? Or perhaps the relationship between the camera and the subject can exist outside these parameters. Whilst these photographs were being taken, were the women looking back at the colonialist, the photographer or indeed just the camera?

The forcible abolition of the veil by Reza Shah in 1936 was met with mixed feeling by Iranian women. For some, the policy was welcome, but for others the move symbolised forced Westernisation by a ruler with little popular support; after Reza Shah's exile in 1941, the veil was reintroduced. Ghazel describes this short period of enforced deveiling as a glitch in Iranian history. For her, Iran has been an Islamic state a great deal longer than not, and she works with the image of the veiled woman as a timeless icon. Ghazel left Iran at the age of nineteen, four years after the Islamic Revolution. She now travels regularly between France and Iran filming her ongoing series *Me*, in which she re-enacts the highlights and lowlights – many ordinary and some extraordinary – from her personal diary, with the veil as her ever-present costume. The appearance of the veil in every episode reduces its significance; it becomes as banal and everyday as it does in any society in which it is omnipresent.

The Iranian landscape, both rural and urban, acts as her stage. She performs each episode in this series – whether it is a ballet lesson, a ski-ing trip, a boxing exercise or hiding during an air raid – with vigour and enthusiasm. These theatrical bursts of energy are full of irony and surreal humour, a cross between a Buster Keaton movie and a Tom and Jerry cartoon. Each scene is accompanied by a qualifying

Overleaf: Marc Garanger,
***Femmes Algériennes* (Algerian Women), 1960. Photographs, 30 x 40cm.**

phrase or sentence in French or English, highlighting her chosen position as outsider and insider, both in and out of Iran.

The development of photography in the Middle East coincided closely with the invention of the medium and, soon after European studios were established in the region, an indigenous art emerged which, despite borrowing heavily from the European photographic tradition, quickly took on a life of its own. Many indigenous photographers even travelled to Europe to exhibit and to develop their skills further. This cross-cultural fertilisation created gaps in the history of the medium in which new and complex developments emerged as fresh and vibrant alternatives to the Orientalist stereotypes found in much of the photography of the period. Despite the ever-shifting political terrain in the Middle East and North Africa, cultural exchange continues to this day, with many artists reclaiming Orientalist icons and placing them back, centre stage, into the landscape of the studio, the desert, the city.

Writing about Sevruguin's work, Ali Behdad notes that:

> Originating in a cultural cross-roads, Sevruguin's photographs reflect the often ambivalent ideologies of that time and place.... Because of the artistic conventions of the time and his audiences' preconceived vision of his subject, Sevruguin borrowed liberally from Orientalism, a borrowing that made some of his photographs affirm popular European conceptions of the Near East.... However Sevruguin's photographs cannot be reduced to a single mode of representation. They demand diverse and contrasting interpretations. Their plural subjects and complex viewpoints encourage us to read them not just along, but often against, written histories of the period and stereotypical representations of place.[9]

Much the same could be said of the works brought together in this publication and exhibition. They have been generated, often with wonderful humour, by artists with an intimate knowledge of both Western and Eastern cultures and some of whom are operating under the codes of Islamic law. Through their work, the artists have helped to broaden the debate on representation and the veil in a complex and provocative way and to sow doubts about the facts of the past, by looking at something we think we know and understand.

Tignous, *Hommage à la Femme Algérienne* (Tribute to Algerian Women), *c.* 1999. Drawing published in *Hors Série Algérie* in the magazine *Télérama*, 21 x 29.7cm. Like some of the artists in the *Veil* exhibition, Tignous uses humour to highlight the condition of Algerian women.

Notes

1. Khemir, Mounira. *The Infinite Image of the Desert and Its Representations*, London: Thames & Hudson, 2000, p. 59.
2. du Camp, Maxime. *Le Nil, Egypte et Nubie*, quoted in Francis Steegmuler, *Flaubert and Madame Bovary*, London: Robert Hale, 1939, p. 196.
3. Graham-Brown, Sarah. *Images of Women: The Portrayal of Women in the Photography of the Middle East 1860–1950*, London: Quartet, 1988, p. 40.
4. The fabrication of the Comtesse and her story adds an interesting twist to the struggle of nineteenth-century European women to establish themselves as careerists in the arts. In her book *Gendering Orientalism: Race, Femininity and Representation* (London: Routledge, 1996), Reina Lewis examines the complex relationships between imperialism, women and culture in the second half of the nineteenth century, drawing particular attention to the work of the Orientalist painter Henriette Browne and the writer George Eliot, neither of whom used their 'real' names.
5. They included Abdullah Frere in Istanbul, Lekegian in Cairo, Kirkorian in Jerusalem and Sevruguin in Tehran.
6. Devereux, Roy. *Aspects of Algeria, Historical, Political, Colonial*, London: J.M. Dent & Sons, 1912, pp. 6–8.
7. Ahmed, Leila. *Edward W. Lane: A Study of His Life and Works and of British Ideas of the Middle East in the Nineteenth Century*, London: Longman, 1978.
8. Alloula, Malek. *The Colonial Harem*, Manchester: Manchester University Press, 1987, p. 14.
9. Bohrer, Frederick N. *Sevruguin and the Persian Image, Photographs of Iran, 1870–1930*. Washington: Arthur M. Sackler Gallery; Seattle and London: University of Washington Press, 1999, p. 95.

The Language of the Veil
Ahdaf Soueif

1923: Stepping down from the train in Cairo Central Station, Hoda Hanim Sha'rawi lifts her hand to the side of her face, undoes a golden clasp, and her fine white crepe-de-chine yashmak flutters to the ground. At that moment, the Turkish-style veil ceased to be de rigueur for Egyptian women of the upper class. Sha'rawi was handsome, wealthy, widowed and securely aristocratic, with powerful political connections through both her father and her husband. She had been in Rome on behalf of the Egyptian Women's Union, a trip that was one more chapter in Egypt's modernisation project. The gesture, at its final moment, resolved a debate that had occupied Egyptian society for almost thirty years.

Or, at least, everyone thought it had. How strange and how telling that now, some eighty years later, here we are talking once more about "the veil". How odd, also, that we don't have one word in Arabic equivalent to "the veil". But perhaps not odd at all, for doesn't English have bowler hats and top hats and trilbys and cloth caps and boaters and stetsons, while Arabic only has *qubba'ah*, "hat"? And when the west – always so inordinately interested in what Arab (or "eastern") women wear – talks about "the veil", doesn't it mysteriously elide the "seductive" veil as worn by, say, Colette in her *Egyptian Tableaux*, and the "forbidding" veil as "forced" on to contemporary eastern women? To the west, "the veil" like Islam itself, is both sensual and puritanical, is contradictory, is to be feared. It is also concrete, and is to do with women, and since cultural battles are so often fought through the bodies of women, it is seized upon by politicians, columnists, feminists....

And so it is that, having refused many times to write about "the veil", I am now trying to put together some thoughts about the "dress code" of Arab or Muslim women. But I immediately run into problems. Muslim women are not all Arab. The conditions of Irani [sic] women are different from those of the women of Pakistan, Turkey, Indonesia and now, famously, Afghanistan. And they are all different from the Arabs. And not all Arab women are Muslim. Thirty years ago, you could not have told whether an Egyptian woman was Christian or Muslim by her dress. In Palestinian villages, you still can't tell. So whose dress code shall I talk about? Where? The clusters of women you see around the shops in Knightsbridge, tented in black, their faces muzzled with leather-and-brass-beaked masks, are from the Gulf states and would (and do) look equally out of place in the shopping malls of Cairo and Beirut. Similarly, the women with layers of black chiffon over their faces and Jimmy Choo slingbacks tripping out from under their black *abayas* are Saudi, and their face coverings send out a different signal from those of an Egyptian or an Algerian. So let us say, for the moment, that we're looking at the dress codes of Egyptian women. Let us further say that the women we will look at will be urban.

In every country, social, cultural and political changes manifest themselves in dress. In Europe, we see this in the loose "Empire" cuts favoured by French ladies after the Revolution, or in the flapper styles that swept England after World War I, or indeed in the miniskirts that came along in the late 1960s with the sexual revolution and the crystallisation of women's lib. None of this is news. And the principle holds for us in the Arab world as well. Except that, in the Arab world, there has been – since the end of the nineteenth century – an additional factor: the powerful presence of the west in our lives and its influence on our social, cultural and political changes. It is interesting, for example, that the Bedouin societies of the Arabian peninsula who came into contact with the west only in the past fifty years or so, and whose contact was essentially political and economic, rather than cultural, and who were also in a position of strength due to their oil, have seen no need for the wholesale adoption of western fashion by their men any more than by their women.

The Language of the Veil
Ahdaf Soueif

Black veil worn by a Saudi woman bearing the Yves Saint-Laurent logo. Photograph: Jodi Cobb, courtesy of the National Geographic Image Collection.

That image of Hoda Sha'rawi unveiling in public was present in the schoolbooks of Nasser's Egypt, and to us – the schoolchildren of the time – the contradiction in it was not immediately apparent. Sha'rawi was part of the struggle to break free from the grip of a European power, yet she publicly adopted the "revealed face" code of that same power. My parents' and grandparents' generations were able to live with this contradiction, because they thought (at least, the ones that thought about it did) that politics and culture existed in two separate realms – that even though we needed to shake off the west's political yoke, the western was the more advanced culture and it was, therefore, progressive to adopt it. As overwrought Arabic narrative forms already in decline gave way to the adopted novel, and the folkloric "shadow-play" transmuted into the three-act drama, as Egyptian sculptors started to exhibit their works and musicians to incorporate waltzes into the traditional Arab quarter tones, so men doffed their *jibbahs* and qaftans and climbed into suits, and women uncovered their faces and hair and donned tailored skirts and jackets and flowered frocks.

A picture I'm looking at now shows a leading Egyptian journalist interviewing Indira Gandhi in 1955. The journalist, Amina al-Sa'id, is wearing a sleeveless, almost off-the-shoulder flowered dress. No one thought anything of it. Yet I'd lay odds that no Egyptian journalist working today would allow herself to be photographed so uncovered. Why? What happened?

Four Women Of Egypt is a brilliant documentary exploring the lives, arguments and friendship of four very different women. At one point, we see stills from the 1960s and 1970s showing Safinaz Kazem, a well-known writer and columnist, svelte and alluring in an assortment of slinky suits and Audrey Hepburn-type shift dresses. Then Kazem, in 1998, in loose clothing and a scarf covering her hair, says, "For years, we ran around in short skirts and bare

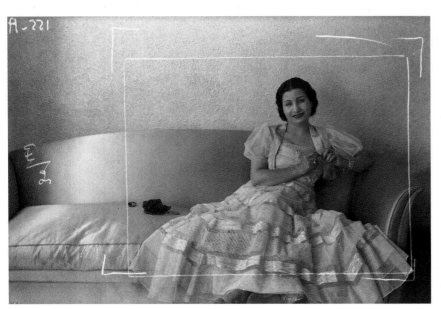

Umm Kalthoum, Cairo, Egypt, 1945-50. Collection: Georges Mikaelaian/FAI. Photograph: Alban. © Fondation Arabe pour l'Image. Kalthoum, like the Egyptian journalist that Soueif describes, is photographed here wearing the latest Western fashions in Egypt in the late 1940s.

arms saying to them, 'Look, see, we're just like you.' Enough. It got us nowhere. We're not like them, and they shouldn't matter. We have to find a way to be ourselves."

It seems it has taken our defeat in the war with Israel in 1967, Nasser's death and Sadat's coming to power in 1970 to bring us back to the position of one of the pioneering feminists, Malak Hifni Nasif, who wrote in 1906 that the veil was, so to speak, a red herring. Her view was that the question of the veil was only central in the debate about women's place in society because the west (personified in Egypt then by Lord Cromer) had made it so. She urged that reformers should concentrate on questions of education, health and economic independence – i.e., the opportunity to work outside the home – and let the veil take care of itself. In the Cairo of the time, women covered their hair with a *tarha*, a thin material in either black or white. For their faces, they had a choice of the white yashmak, which was drawn across the face under the eyes and connoted the aristocracy and their imitators; the *bisha*, which could be casually thrown over the whole face and was neutral in class terms; and the *burqu'*, a rectangle of the same fabric as fishnet stockings that was hung from under the eyes with a small decorative gold or brass cylinder at its centre over the nose. This last was very much the accessory of the *bint al-balad*, the "native woman" of the working or lower middle class, who had no desire to imitate the yashmak- or *bisha*-wearing ladies. It is, of course, different from the Afghani "burka", and would not have afforded much of a disguise in the Simpson & Ridley antics.

When I was growing up in the 1960s, the *tarha* was generally worn by women of the working class and by traditional women over, say, fifty of all classes. The *burqu'* could still be glimpsed as a piece of exotica in some popular districts of Cairo, but the *bisha* and the yashmak were to be found only in sepia photographs.

1971: Until the early 1970s, if you sat in the Cafe Riche on Qasr el-Nil Street watching the world go by, you could tell fairly accurately what a person was by their clothes. And, generally, the more affluent a person was, the more westernised they looked. That woman there, the slim one in the well-cut suit with the skirt just above the knee, in sunglasses; she might be an engineer/doctor/lawyer/academic/ranking civil servant, or married to one; or she may own one of the new boutiques that have started appearing as Sadat yanks the reins sharply right towards a capitalist, open-door economy. That child hurrying across the street in slippers and an ill-fitting dress with a white kerchief binding her hair is a servant-girl, sent out to fetch something in a hurry. And here come two women deep in conversation – one has her hair covered in a kind of filigree bonnet, the other wears hers in a bun; they walk slowly in their sensible shoes, and they wear what most Cairene women wear: a straight, dark gabardine skirt ending just below the knee and over it a shirt in a floral or geometric pattern with an open collar and sleeves just above the elbow. They are (or are married to) minor civil servants, schoolteachers or legal workers, but they might also be the wives of men in trade, or workers in the large public sector factories: textiles, pharmaceuticals, food, steel and so on. In other words, they are either the petty bourgeoisie or the upwardly mobile working class. As for that comely, plump woman hurrying along, her long, black overdress similar to that of the peasant woman, her head covered in a loose black transparent *tarha* over the flowered scarf that binds her hair, she might be married to a butcher's or grocer's assistant, she might work as a cleaner in a school or a hospital or a government office.

Men pass, too, but we ignore them as we watch a bevy of young women saunter by in skirts above the knee and jeans, in tight jumpers and silver bracelets, their hair flowing on their shoulders or cut short

Emily Jacir, *From Paris to Riyadh (Drawings for my Mother)*, 1998–2001. Installation shot and detail, marker on vellum, 24 x 28cm. Photographs: Emily Jacir.

comme les garçons. These are students from one of Cairo's various universities, arts academies and colleges.

If we're watching closely, the silver bracelets should tell us something, for since the mid-1960s there has been a revival of interest in traditional culture. Folkloric dance troupes have been formed, the Arab Music Ensemble plays to packed houses, motifs from Egyptian epics find their way into the three-act dramas, the comfortably-off are ordering bits of *mashrabiyya* and appliqué tapestries for their homes (to the relief of the craftsmen, who were dying out fast) and the fashionable silver jewellery blends pharaonic design with inscriptions of classical Arabic poetry. Some women artists, such as the documentary film-maker Atiyyat al-Abnudi, in the absence of a national costume, adopt a modified version of the peasant woman's smocked and colourful *galabiyyas*, getting them made up in pure cottons or rich velvets.

2001: Thirty years have passed as we take our seats today at the Cafe Riche, which – thank goodness – is still there: Qasr el-Nil Street throngs with three times more people than it did on that October afternoon long ago, and the daughters of those women we watched then are having a harder time getting through the crowds. Most of the women struggling to keep a foothold on the pavement are in a variant of the old uniform: the straight gabardine skirt is now just above the ankles, the patterned shirt is longer, and now has long sleeves. The head is covered with a scarf folded into a large, concealing triangle.

This has become the "default" dress. In the 1970s, the regime of President Anwar Sadat did three things: it switched the Egyptian economy from socialist to capitalist and opened the door to foreign investment, it signed a peace treaty with Israel and, to weaken the opposition critical of both these policies, it nurtured and funded the political Islamist groups. The sky-high inflation resulting from the economic policy and the corruption that came along with it led whoever could to head for the oil-rich Arab states, thus opening the way for their brand of puritanical Islam to enter Egypt. The ones who did not leave – the majority of the population – became increasingly disenfranchised, hard-up and angry; except, that is, for the very, very few who were making money rapidly.

The treaty with Israel, when it was not followed by a just settlement for the Palestinians, and even though it won back the Sinai for Egypt, generated more anger still; except, that is, for the very, very few who developed vested interests with Israel. Both these policies – involving, as they did, a turning-away from the Soviet Union – were perceived as western-backed. So people questioned whether following the west was good for Egypt. Perhaps, they thought, we should look back at ourselves, at our own history and traditions, and find the way forward there. Sadat's third policy ensured that the anger and questioning had no outlet, no platform or expression except the Islamist one. Covering her hair then started as a woman's act of political protest and a symbol of a search for an Egyptian, non-westernised identity. In two decades, it became simply what you did – unless you took a conscious decision not to.

Many young women in the street today are in *hijab*: a long, loose garment topped with a large plain scarf securely fastened so no hair, ears or neck show through. Some wear it because they believe this is what a good Muslim woman should wear, and, they add, why should men who are not entitled look at my hair or my figure? It neutralises, they say, men's tendency to look at women as sex objects. Some wear it because it deals with the economic problem posed by the need to wear different outfits for different occasions, and makes you a good Muslim into the bargain. Some wear it because their friends are wearing it and they don't want to stand out, and if their friends think it makes you a good Muslim, well, why not?

Majida Khattari, *Les Mille et Une Souffrances de Tchadiri* (1001 Sufferings of Tchadiri), no. 7, 2001. Blue and green stretch cotton with fishing net. Photograph by Majida Khattari.

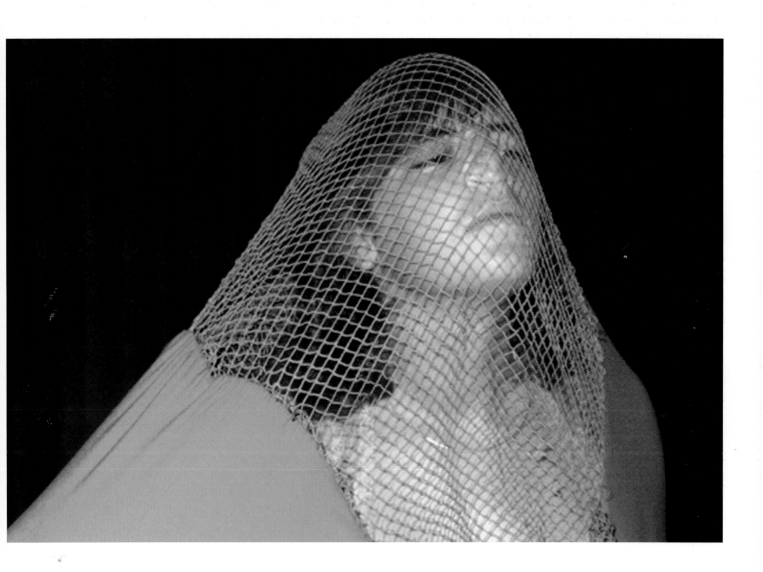

Today, I see only one woman in the full *niqab*, a black *hijab* outfit with a thick, black cloth over the face and a narrow slit to see through. She hurries along, her every movement as deliberate as her garb, which says loud and clear: "I am a political Islamist. I believe our only solution lies in creating an Islamic state. I am in opposition to this government." It takes guts to do this in these days of arbitrary detentions and torture. Guts, or desperation.

Tyres shriek. A woman has started to cross the street and is almost run over by a speeding Cherokee. The driver leans out of the window. Her hair is expensively streaked and her lip-linered mouth screams at the pedestrian: "Open your eyes, you backward one." She wears an imitation tiger-skin top, and if she were to step out of the car we would see that she is in boots and leather trousers. In the back seat there is a small Filipino nanny, which means that her daughter, in Gap jeans in the passenger seat, probably does not speak Arabic. This is the family of one of the businessmen who have made it big in the new economic climate.

The woman who was almost run over adjusts her headscarf and dusts down her brown gabardine skirt. She mutters something about "the pashas of these sooty times" and passers-by shake their heads in sympathy. She is a teacher married to an architect. Unable to make ends meet in the inflation-ridden 1970s, they had migrated to Kuwait, but were asked to leave after the Gulf War. They lost their savings in the collapse of the big Islamist investment companies, and are now more or less back where they started. There are many, many like her. Where do they go from here?

For at least four thousand years, Egyptian women have understood the power of the image and have, when they could, manipulated it to their advantage. Nefertiti, reigning with her husband Akhenatun as the first co-monarch, had herself depicted as the Goddess Isis, a PR coup to be followed by Cleopatra some fourteen centuries later when she made her triumphal entry into Rome as Caesar's honoured guest. In more modern times, Shahindah Maqlad, who presented herself as a traditional beauty in her portrait of 1953, transformed herself in 1966 into a modern "woman of the people" as she demanded that the murder of her husband (allegedly) by a feudal family be investigated. And Rawiyah Atiyyah, running for elections after Suez (or, as we know it, the Port-Said War) created an icon by celebrating her victory in battle fatigues.

So what do we do now? The image we need to project should embody our Egyptian notion of ourselves at this moment. It should also appeal to the audience. But we are multiple and varied, and who's sitting in the dress circle? Many think there's no longer any point in playing to the west. And there is no Second Power. And – until the bombing of Afghanistan – political Islam had lost credibility in the Egyptian street. If only we had a national costume, such as a sari or a *sirwal qamis*, a lot of us would probably be wearing it right now.

First published in *The Guardian*, weekend supplement, 8 December 2001, pp. 29–32.

Majida Khattari, *Kacha* (Cover), 1996. Felt sewn with wire, hoops and strips of elastic over the head. Photograph taken at the fashion show in Arles during the International Festival of Photography in 1998 by François Mallinjod.

Visibility, Violence and Voice? Attitudes to Veiling Post-11 September
Alison Donnell

11 September 2001 has become known, in media-speak at least, as the day that changed the world, but whose world did it change, in what ways and to what effects? Most obviously, the bombing of the twin towers of the World Trade Center changed America's world, bringing terrorist violence back home, but it also changed the world of Afghanistan on whom war was declared and cluster bombs rained. But if the experience of violence, insecurity, grief and dismay were newly inscribed upon contemporary America, for Afghanistan they had long been daily realities. The events following 11 September have – in bold and frightening ways – shown majority populations living in Europe and the United States what is at stake in claiming allegiance to a nation, a religion, or an identity and what is at stake in declaring difference too. However, the high stakes and daily experience of living under a regime in which allegiance and identity are policed with both vigour and violence have been the reality for people living in Afghanistan for many years.

As well as revealing the alliance between al-Qaida and the Taliban; the desperate situation of Afghan citizens, both those living in Afghanistan and those displaced in refugee camps; and the particular crimes being perpetrated against women, the events of 11 September disclosed the extent to which American media groups control issues of political visibility and invisibility. In his 1981 book *Covering Islam: How the Media and the Experts Determine How We See the Rest of the World*, Edward Said carefully and powerfully demonstrates the political currency of American representations of Islam in moments of political crisis and unpacks the imbalanced and biased views that masquerade as historical reality and objective reportage. Post-11 September, a political situation and a human rights crisis that had been happening, and known to be happening, for many years was suddenly and strategically made media-visible.

In the television documentary, *Behind the Veil* that was shown to British audiences in June 2001 and to American audiences in late August 2001, Saira Shah, a British-born Afghan, entered Afghanistan undercover to film and narrate a piece which documents in graphic and harrowing detail the human rights abuses and in particular the sanctioned violence against women under the Taliban. Despite Shah's own conviction about the need to draw international attention to the situation in Afghanistan, in an interview with CNN just weeks before 11 September, Shah pointed out:

> Afghanistan used to be important, but so many things have happened there, and things have happened because Afghanistan was used as a pawn in the '80s. There is now no international interest in Afghanistan. People have to care about Afghanistan around the world, and maybe a head of steam will be built that can do some good.[1]

Although 11 September provided a scalding head of steam, it is not so easy to decide whether it has resulted in any 'good', or provoked a new global ethic of care. Indeed, if Afghan women are now receiving the kinds of international attention that many had worked and hoped for, then it has to be noted that they are doing so very much on the West's terms.

It is neither surprising nor incidental that media coverage of Afghanistan post-11 September relied heavily on the veil as an effective visual shorthand which draws on dress codes already naturalised within the West as emblematic of oppression. However, it may be possible to argue that the over-determined and over-simplified representation of the veil in Western cultures has been thrown into a different floodlight post-11 September, one that casts new and ominous political shadows. The familiar and much-analysed Orientalist gaze through which the veil is viewed as

Visibility, Violence and Voice? Attitudes to Veiling Post-11 September
Alison Donnell

an object of mystique, exoticism and eroticism and the veiled woman as an object of fantasy, excitement and desire is now replaced by the xenophobic, more specifically Islamophobic, gaze through which the veil, or headscarf, is seen as a highly visible sign of a despised difference. In the immediate aftermath of 11 September, so severe and immediate was the threat to veiled women in America, that *imams* published affirmative *fatwas* in *al-Majalla* magazine allowing women to remove their scarves in public. America's Muslim Women's League published similar advice in an article entitled 'Muslim Dress in Dangerous Times':

In the current climate of escalated religiously-motivated violence since the terrible attacks of September 11, Muslim women in hijab (headscarf) are particularly vulnerable because, for many years, western media and literature have consistently portrayed covered women as the predominant image of Islam. As a result, Muslim women in headscarves and other Muslim-style clothing are often the first and easiest targets of hate violence. American Muslim women should keep all this in mind as they decide how to dress in the next weeks and months. If a Muslim woman senses a possible danger to herself, adjusting her attire to minimize the chances of physical attack is a logical and Islamically permissible precaution that falls squarely within the fiqh principles of necessity and hardship. Whatever one ultimately feels is the best attire for a Muslim woman, the Quran is also clear that Islamic dress is something to help us avoid harassment (Quran 33:59)....
In such situations, individual life and personal safety take precedence over normal Islamic rules. As established in a primary principle of Islamic jurisprudence, "*necessity renders the forbidden permissible.*" (Said Ramadan, Islamic Law: Its Scope and Equity 71 [1970]).[2]

Indeed, so transparent was the link between veiling and abuse that in order to express support for Muslim women, an interfaith peace group established a 'Scarves for Solidarity' campaign and asked non-Muslim women to wear scarves on 8 October 2001, also warning them to expect hostility. In a British context, forms of identification also became less mobile and with the consolidation of populations into the categories of known and unknown, insiders and outsiders, the veil served as a declaration of difference. Far from affording women the kind of visual immunity that is part of its intended function, the veil, and those who wore it, now became the subject of acute public interest. A special feature entitled 'The Other Side of the Veil' in *The Guardian Weekend* on 8 December 2001 declared: 'Since September 11, the world's focus has been on Islam as never before – and women are at the heart of it.' Reporting on her meeting with a group of Muslim women at the ArRum club in London, Madeleine Bunting first comments on the dress of the Muslim women she meets, and then their beliefs, 'All have chosen in the past few years to wear the *hijab*.... Most strikingly, however, all of these women fluently and cogently articulate how they believe Islam has liberated and empowered them.'[3] The words 'most strikingly' indicate the surprise, perhaps even disbelief, that the terms of dress and religious affiliation she is greeted with are harmonious with the promotion of freedom for women. In fact, for at least one of these women it was the decision to adopt *hijab* and take up full religious observance that gave her the confidence and knowledge to insist on her rights to a university education and avoid an arranged marriage. Although this article clearly demonstrates the pressure that the veil exerts on Western understandings of freedom, it does not address this issue directly, unlike a recent article, 'The Veil in my Handbag', by Aisha Khan. For Khan post-11 September, being British and being Muslim are virtually mutually exclusive identities:

You can be born and raised in this country, benefit from its education and live freely and comfortably thanks to the solid British economy. But you can also be oppressed. Stay silent when your religion is being lambasted in the press. Look on helplessly when Muslims are being persecuted in their homeland and then watch them being punished by the British asylum system. Stuff your veil into your handbag because you'll never get that job if you cover your head. Sacrifice prayer times and fasting to keep up with the crowd and stay in with the boss.[4]

And yet, while the veil marked women in the West as targets of both direct and subtle forms of abuse, Western media representation emblematised both the alterity and the repression of women in Afghanistan through their veiling.

Although the physical restrictions and social limitations that being forced to wear the burka imposes on women should not be underestimated, it does appear that the visual privileging of veiling has narrowed the focus on women's rights. Indeed, the veil is so easily translated into a visual vocabulary of oppression that it is difficult to divert attention on to the more pressing issues for women in many Muslim countries, such as their legal status in issues relating to custody, inheritance and testimony. The veiled figure also serves to fix Afghan women as hidden and passive and therefore enacts an ideological barrier conditioning expectations of victimhood rather than of voice. Even those pieces of journalism and personal narratives which do speak out about other issues usually deploy veiled figures as their 'illustration' and make reference to the veil in their title; albeit unwittingly, they are thereby confirming the centrality of the veil to any fuller discussion.

A cursory glance at a cluster of publications on and by women in Afghanistan that have appeared post-11 September registers the persistence of the veil.

Several life narratives of women who have left Afghanistan have been published; all describe terrible personal sufferings as well as the affliction of other women under the Taliban, but they also narrate these women's ability to stage resistance and to escape. Despite the differences between the protagonists and their stories, the covers of three separate books – Siba Shakib, *Afghanistan: Where God Only Comes to Weep*; Zoya with John Follain and Rita Cristofari, *Zoya's Story: An Afghan Woman's Battle for Freedom*; and Latifa with Chékéha Hachemi, *My Forbidden Face* – all show a woman or women wearing the burka. This very same image covers M.E. Hirsh's *Kabul*, Cheryl Benard and Edit Schlaffer's *Veiled Courage: Inside the Afghan Women's Resistance*, and also, most ironically, Harriet Logan's *Unveiled: Voices of Women in Afghanistan*. The last two titles feature interviews and photographs of women engaged in resistant education and healthcare work, while all of these works testify to the possibilities of struggle and the agency of Afghan women. The persistent circulation of visual images of veiled Afghan women seems to suggest that George W. 'Bush's war' has translated their status from that of indifference into that of difference. Moreover, while there is no denying that the situation of Afghan women has become newsworthy since 11 September, it is not always easy to decide whether the coverage has helped to campaign for social justice or has simply reiterated simplistic assumptions, stereotyped representations and political justifications for continued Western military intervention in the Middle East.

It is interesting that it was on the issue of women's rights in Afghanistan that both Laura Bush, the First Lady of the United States, and Cherie Blair, the wife of the British Prime Minister, claimed their own political voices. On 17 November 2001, Laura Bush took up her husband's customary radio slot to address the nation; the terms of her address are significant in that she positions her husband's war on terrorism as a means of 'saving' Afghan women:

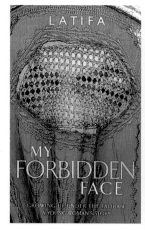

Front cover of Latifa's *My Forbidden Face. Growing Up Under the Taliban: A Young Woman's Story* (London: Virago Press, 2002).

Mohsen Makhmalbaf, *Kandahar*,
2001. Film still. © WildBunch.
Released shortly after
11 September, *Kandahar* tells
the story of a young woman
journalist's journey to rescue her
sister in the city of Kandahar.
The protagonist's frustration
at having to wear a burka is
portrayed in depth in the film.

Because of our recent military gains in much of Afghanistan, women are no longer imprisoned in their homes. They can listen to music and teach their daughters without fear of punishment. Yet the terrorists who helped rule that country now plot and plan in many countries. And they must be stopped. The fight against terrorism is also a fight for the rights and dignity of women.[5]

While Laura Bush may have been right in her accusations of cruelty and violence perpetrated against women since 1996 and the imposition of Taliban rule, her speech confirmed the image of Afghan women as victims. Just days later, it was precisely this image that Cherie Blair drew attention to when, having listened to a group of Afghan women refugees at a gathering which she hosted, she too spoke out. Her focus was rather different to that of Laura Bush and seemed more concerned with alerting the West to the ways in which Afghan women can help rebuild their nation in alliance with Britain:

> The women here prove that the women of Afghanistan still have a spirit that belies their unfair, downtrodden image. We need to help them free that spirit and give them their voice back, so they can create the better Afghanistan we all want to see.[6]

Given this emphasis upon women's agency and voice in spite of repression, it is particularly significant that Cherie Blair's words are reported in an article entitled 'Beyond the Burka' and are given about a third of the half-page spread, while the remaining two-thirds are dedicated to a striking photograph of Mrs Blair imaginatively reconstructing what it might be like to have only peepholes on the world.

In all contexts it is clear that there has been less attention to women's resistance, agency and organised opposition to the Taliban regime than to the imposition of the veil. There are a wide range of women's organisations including the Revolutionary Association of the Women of Afghanistan (RAWA), the Afghan Women's Council, Afghan Women's Skills Development Center, Humanitarian Assistance for the Women and Children of Afghanistan, the Afghan Women's Network, and the Afghan Women's Resource Center. Indeed, these organisations, as well as disseminating many troubling images and narratives of women's oppression under the Taliban, also offer a corrective perspective to the simplistic view of the Afghan veiled woman as victim through their persistent, productive and courageous efforts to establish medical centres, schools and other forms of support. Such activities were highlighted pre-11 September by the launching of the RAWA

Cherie Blair, wife of Britain's Prime Minister, Tony Blair, holds her hands to her eyes as she chats to women from Afghanistan about the traditional burka at 10 Downing Street in London on Monday 19 November 2001.
© Associated Press/Pool.
Photograph by Ian Waldie/Pool.

website in March 2001; by Shah's documentary; and by many other pieces of journalism, scholarship and personal testimony. What is signified by the fact that post-11 September they acquired a new political validity and a new global audience?

RAWA's website crashed as a result of overload when it was cited on *The Oprah Winfrey Show* on 5 October 2001. However, it is important to note that the show itself did not foreground the agency and potentiality of Afghan women demonstrated by RAWA and other groups, but rather devoted most of the airtime, supposedly dedicated to an introduction and explanation of Islam, to a discussion of *hijab*. Again, the veil or scarf became the focal point. Discussing the way in which the programme intended to take up the urgent challenge of introducing and explaining Islam to the American public only to be derailed by a focus on *hijab*, Afra Jalabi argues that the veil has now become a tool of political distraction. For Jalabi, the veil is a false centre to discussions of social justice and a highly charged symbol of difference that paralyses productive cross-cultural debate and communication:

> But did we discuss the meaning of being Muslim, or the problem of violence, or even the rage caused by American foreign policy in the region? No, the Muslim audience had more pressing

RAWA rally in Islamabad, 28 April 2000. © RAWA/ World Picture News.

things to discuss. The show proved to be a mirror of our intellectual bankruptcy, a mirror of our true obsessions and fixations, because after a quick discussion of what Islam was about, the show veered off to discuss women in Islam, particularly the dress code. The 'after show' segment, which the program puts daily on its website after the live recording in the studio, was entirely about 'Hijab.' This was both insightful and disheartening. It seemed that the gender question in Islam had become the central issue and what Muslim women wear the core of the debate on Islam, both internally and externally. It was disgraceful to see how our contemporary discourse as 'modern Muslims' has become so focused on the scarf at the expense of the real paradigms that define Islam, its history and its universal values.[7]

With more specific focus on the situation of women in Afghanistan, Adeena Niazi, one of two hundred women delegates to attend the 1,600-strong congregation of the *loya jirga* (grand council) in Kabul in June 2002 also wanted to argue against the determined concentration on veiling: 'Having a burqa or not having a burqa does not guarantee our safety... the key issue for women is security and safety; women want to wake up and not be afraid that they or their children will be kidnapped or raped.'[8]

Indeed, it is important to ask whether veiling has not only been used to simplify the issues regarding the position of women in Afghanistan before 11 September, but also to distort their situation almost a year hence. If the images of women taking off their veils and men shaving off their beards have been described as 'the most joyous journalistic images of 2001' and constructed to offer a promise of liberation and a politics of hope, do such images equate with a new just politics and gender equality in Afghanistan?[9] RAWA has already registered its dissatisfaction at

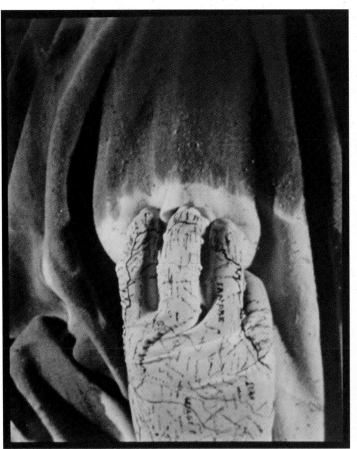

Ramesh Kalkur, *Untitled*, 1996.
Photographs, 50 x 60cm.

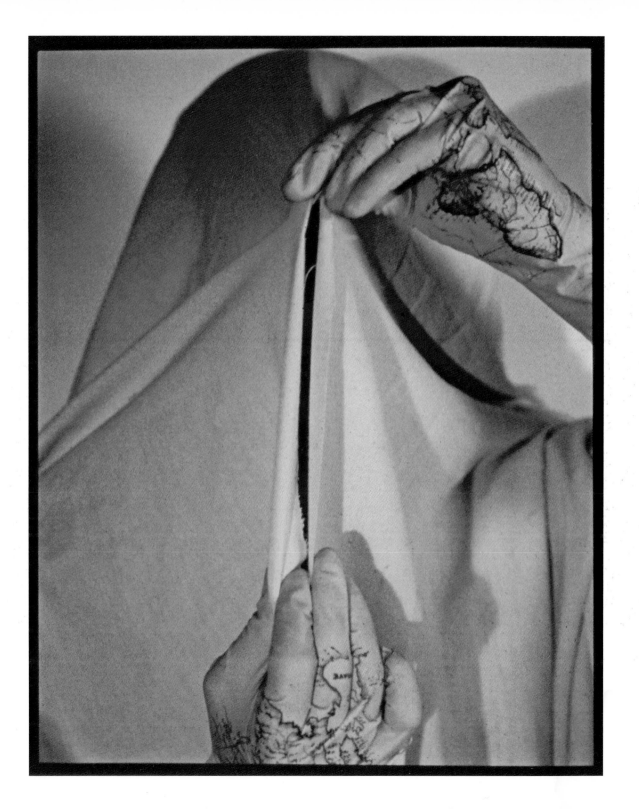

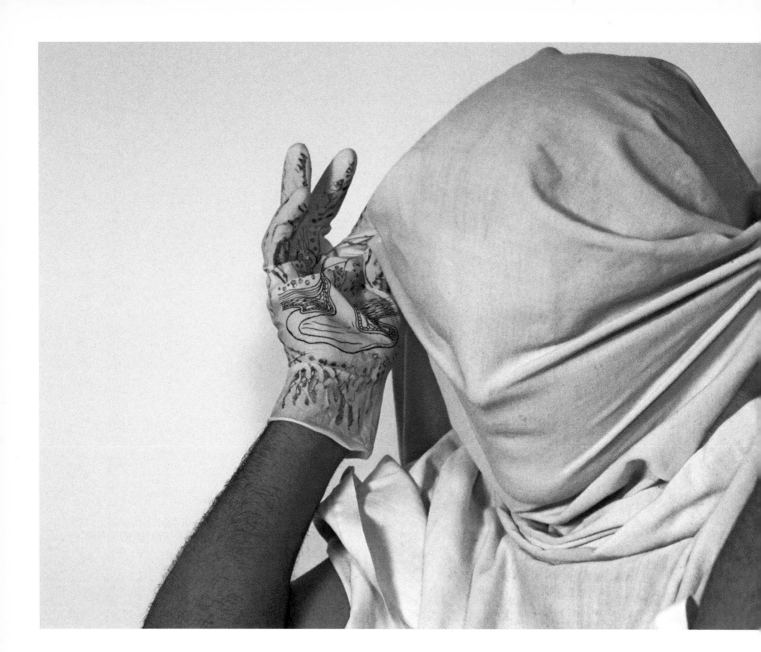

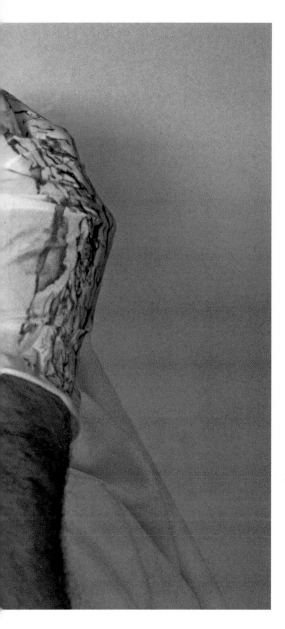

Ramesh Kalkur, *Untitled,* **1996.**
Photograph, 60 x 31.5cm.

power being given to the Northern Alliance who engaged in mass violence during their rule from 1992–96. In an article for *The Guardian* in March 2002, one of its members, Mariam Rawi, commented that:

We are receiving numerous reports of rape, looting and kidnapping from across the country. Those who have proclaimed women's liberation have spoken far too soon. Widespread fear of the Alliance means few women have discarded their burqas. Hundreds of thousands of school-age girls are unable to attend lessons due to destitution, insecurity, and the fallout of a decade of fundamentalist oppression.[10]

Although international attention has clearly been problematic in its choice of subject and its strategic representations of suffering and political change, there is anxiety about what will happen to women in Afghanistan once such attention has waned. The violation of women's rights has been an integral part of the West's justification of the 'liberation' – by means of the destruction – of Afghanistan. Once this project is over, what hope is there for a long-term interest in human rights? What is to prevent the reality of Melika Brown's shocking comment, 'If Romanian babies were the Nineties' pet cause, then oppressed Afghan women must be this decade's equivalent.'[11]

The most complex and urgent questions around veiling, such as the need to differentiate, historicise and locate women's own creative and differing responses to the veil, as well as the issue of rights in relation to compulsory unveiling, are the subject of many scholarly debates.[12] Nevertheless, the differences in social conditions and political status enjoyed by different communities of veiled women and the many cultural variables and specificities that attend the wearing of veils are seldom the interest of those who represent the veiled woman to and for the West. Even the word 'veil' implies the fixing and homogenising of a range of dress practices and garments which are worn in accordance with *hijab*. In Egypt today, where the full continuum between Western dress, the *tarha*, *hijab* and *niqab* can be seen on the streets, these garments not only serve to signify the choice of Western or non-Western forms of identification, but also class position and political allegiance. However, practices in Egypt are different from those in Indonesia, the world's largest Muslim population. In countries bordering the Persian Gulf, including Saudi Arabia, Iran and Yemen, even non-Muslim women must wear veils and yet the Taliban regime prevented foreign women from wearing the burka, thus consciously displaying them as Other.

The multiple functions and values of the veil also need to be acknowledged. For some women, the veil empowers them by removing their bodies from male scrutiny and the social judgments of beauty and sexuality and they wear it by choice. For others, enforced veiling is a political oppression disconnected from Islam, as experienced in Afghanistan by Latifa: 'I climb out of the burqa feeling humiliated and furious. My face belongs to me. The Koran says that a woman can be veiled, but that she must remain recognizable. The Taliban want to steal my face, forbid us all faces.'[13] Veiling can also be a conscious drawing attention to oneself – not as a beautiful or sexual being – but as a political one. In 'Algeria Unveiled', Frantz Fanon documents how in relation to Algeria's struggle for independence the veil was 'transformed into a technique of camouflage, into a means of struggle'.[14] Fanon not only refers here to the pragmatic value of a garment that conceals arms and confers anonymity but also to the struggle for ideological identification in which the veil represents the wilful abrogation of Western values.

Post-11 September, it would appear that attitudes to and representations of the veil have overwhelmingly

Studio Photograph, Saida, Lebanon, c. 1955. Photograph by Chafic el Soussi, collection FAI. © Fondation Arabe pour l'Image. Here – together with an elaborate hairstyle, make-up and jewelry – the veil is worn to decorative effect, to create a glamorous and seductive appearance.

demonstrated the intransigence of the veiled woman as an icon of oppression – an embodiment of the rationale for the continuation of George W. Bush's war without end, a strategic figure constantly evoked as a visual reminder of the incommensurability between Western and Islamic societies. Even in those instances where the exposure given to Afghan women has occasioned a coming to voice, the contradictions and complexities within their realities and their narratives that unpick the tightly fastened seams between the veil and oppression, Islam and religious fundamentalism are not the aspects that are highlighted or explored.

As my analysis of various forms of representation demonstrates, the veiled woman tends to be used to engineer a representational equivalence between the Islamic woman and a cloistered, apolitical, even ahistorical victim. Yet if 11 September 2001 has failed to bring attention to the diversity, agency and political activity of women in Islamic societies, despite significant evidence of the remarkable and daring work of many women's organisations, perhaps the events of 31 January 2002 will succeed. On that day, the spurious notion that women in Islam remain outside the world of political alliances and military strikes was perhaps most dramatically exploded by the actions of Wafa Idrees, the first woman Palestinian suicide bomber, who killed one Israeli and injured 140 others in a Jerusalem street. In her twenties, Idrees was working as an emergency medical volunteer with the Palestinian Red Crescent and witnessed many of the casualties of the clashes in Ramallah. She was known to be both distressed and frustrated at the situation she encountered first hand and yet there were expressions of surprise at her action, in part motivated by her mode of dress and appearance. A news report pointed out: 'She did not fit the usual profile of a suicide bomber. Family pictures show her wearing makeup and sleeveless dresses. "She was not religious, she didn't pray and didn't cover up," [a friend] said.'[15] What can we learn from the horrific situation of a woman who gained equality and served as an iconoclast of Islamic womanhood at the terrible cost of her own life?

If Palestine is a major protagonist in the continued war between the Middle East and the West of which 11 September may be seen as a terrible and defining moment, then it is perhaps through paying just and careful attention to the situation of Palestine that the West can learn to disabuse itself of naive and damaging notions of Islamic societies and the shorthand distortions which the media encourages. Given the continued plight of women in Afghanistan and the desperation of Palestinian suicide bombers (not to mention the situation in Iraq and the Sudan), there is clearly a political urgency to the project of revisiting preconceptions and prejudices concerning many aspects of Islam, as well as to that of differentiating and understanding the various populations and nations which identify themselves as Islamic.

The concentration on the veil in Western discussions of Islamic societies can legitimately be seen to divert attention from other issues such as legal rights, education and access to healthcare. However, given the fact that attitudes to the veil post-11 September have only confirmed Chandra Talpade Mohanty's proposal that the 'veiled woman' is one of the 'universal images of "the third-world" woman... setting in motion a colonialist discourse which exercises a very specific power in defining, coding and maintaining existing first/third world connections', then any serious and sustained attempts to interrogate, destabilise and reconstruct the political biases which inform acts of representing the veil may be a useful and significant starting point from which to redefine the terms of the 'insider/outsider' divide that 11 September all too often and disappointingly provoked.[16] In the light of political failure, perhaps cultural interventions can bring change to the pattern through which Muslim women only achieve Western visibility by suffering violence.

Notes

1. 'Journalist Saira Shah: Life in Afghanistan under the Taliban', 27 August 2001 (www.cnn.com/2001/COMMUNITY/08/24/shah/index.html).

2. Muslim Women's League, 'Women's Dress in Dangerous Times' (www.mwlusa.org/hijab_dangerous_times.htm).

3. Bunting, Madeleine. 'Can Islam Liberate Women?', in *The Guardian Weekend*, 8 December 2001, p. 16.

4. Khan, Aisha. 'The Veil in My Handbag', in *The Guardian*, 18 June 2002. (Aisha Khan is a pseudonym.)

5. www.whitehouse.gov/news/releases/2001/11/20011117.html

6. Ward, Lucy. 'Beyond the Burka', in *The Guardian*, 20 November 2001, p. 4.

7. Jalabi, Afra. 'To Veil or Not to Veil, That is the Question' (www.mwlusa.org/hijab_oprah.htm).

8. Mackinnon, Mark. 'Afghan Women Take Historic Step in Kabul', in *The Globe and Mail*, 13 June 2002.

9. Gardener, Marilyn. 'Lifting the Veil on Women's Subjugation', in *Christian Science Monitor*, 28 November 2001.

10. Rawi, Mariam. 'Burqa Still a Symbol of Fear', in *The Guardian*, 7 March 2002. See also the Human Rights Watch briefing paper 'Taking Cover: Women in Post-Taliban Afghanistan' (http://hrw.org/backgrounder/wrd/afghan-women-2k2.htm).

11. Brown, Melika. Review of *Zoya's Story: An Afghan Woman's Battle for Freedom*, in *The Times*, 20 April 2002.

12. See Blank and Göcek in 'The Veil: Postcolonialism and the Politics of Dress', in Alison Donnell (ed.), *Interventions: International Journal of Postcolonial Studies*, London: Routledge, vol. 1, no. 4.

13. Latifa, *My Forbidden Face*, London: Virago, 2002, p. 41.

14. Fanon, Frantz. *Studies in a Dying Colonialism*, rev. ed., London: Earthscan Publications, 1989, p. 61.

15. 'Unthinkable Actions: Woman's Apparent Suicide Bombing Makes Israelis Suspect All Palestinians', 31 January 2002 (http://more.abcnews.go.com/sections/world/dailynews/mideast020130.html).

16. Mohanty, Chandra Talpade, 'Under Western Eyes: Power, Representation and Feminist Critique', in Mohanty, Chandra Talpade, Ann Russo and Lourdes Torres (eds.), *Third World Women and the Politics of Feminism*, Bloomington: Indiana University Press, 1991, p. 73.

**Poetics and Politics of Veil,
Voice and Vision in Iranian
Post-revolutionary Cinema**
Hamid Naficy

In the early 1990s, a journalist in Paris asked renowned Iranian film-maker Abbas Kiarostami to evaluate the status of the current Iranian cinema. With a mixture of pride and sly satisfaction, Kiarostami answered: 'I think of it as one of Iran's major exports: in addition to pistachio nuts, carpets, and oil, now there is cinema.'[1] Described as 'one of the pre-eminent national cinemas in the world today' by both Toronto International Film Festival and New York Film Festival, Iranian cinema is a new, vital cinema with its own special industrial and financial structure, and unique politics and poetics. It is also part of a more general transformation in the political culture of the country since the anti-Shah revolution of 1978–79, which brought the current Islamic regime to power.

A unique and unexpected achievement of this cinema has been the significant and signifying role of women both behind and in front of the camera, leading to 'women's cinema'. However, this is by no means a cohesive movement with its own unique ideology, aesthetics, politics, funding structure and spectators. Rather, the rise of differently situated women directors is emblematic and constitutive of the forceful emergence of women into the public space in many spheres, including politics, cinema, television, press, and performing and visual arts. Nonetheless, there are certain shared structures that undergird women's films and certain common aesthetic features, which give rise to the notion of a women's cinema. Among these are the political and financial structures of the film industry and the manner in which the social rules of modesty and veiling (*hijab* in its widest sense) and gendered segregation of space are institutionalised in the industry. Among the aesthetic features are the ways that modesty and gendered spatiality are inscribed in the films. This essay deals with the process by which these politics and poetics of modesty and veiling were institutionalised, resisted and incorporated into the film industry and film texts and the way

they evolved over the years toward liberal and counterhegemonic interpretations. Particular emphasis is placed on the works of key women film-makers.

An extraordinary fact of Iranian post-revolution cinema is that more women feature-film directors emerged in a single decade after the revolution than existed in all the country's preceding eight decades of film-making – and this in a patriarchal and traditional society ruled by an Islamist ideology that is highly suspicious of the corruptive influence of cinema on women and of women on cinema. Prior to the revolution, only one woman, Shahla Riahi, had directed a feature film (*Marjan*, 1956). Today, a dozen women – all of whom have emerged since the revolution – are directing feature fiction films.[2] And there are many who direct documentaries, television series and serials, short subject films and animated films. This achievement was partly made possible by the incorporation of a complex system of modesty at all levels of the motion picture industry and in the cinematic texts. A major goal of this system was to disrupt the direct discursive link between the representation of women and the promotion of corruption, amorality and pornography which the pre-revolution cinema was said to have established. To that end it became necessary for the post-revolutionary government to strengthen two existing discourses: the 'injection' theory of cinematic power and the 'realist illusionist' theory of cinematic representation. The injection theory posited that the mere exposure to unveiled or immodest women would turn autonomous and moral individuals (particularly men) into dependent, deceived and corrupt subjects. The realist illusionist theory insisted on a direct and unmediated correspondence between reality and its representation (or illusion) on the screen. For the illusion to be Islamically modest, reality had to become (or to be made to appear) modest. This necessitated a total and widespread process of purification to cleanse

Poetics and Politics of Veil, Voice and Vision in Iranian Post-revolutionary Cinema
Hamid Naficy

the film industry, the cinemas and the cinema screens of the offending vices and corruption.[3] The result was that the industry became open to women directors and the cinemas to women audiences, as long as women abided by very specific and binding Islamic codes of modesty and gender segregation.

Self, Modesty and Gender Segregation

In many non-Western societies with strong hierarchical and collective relationships, including Iran, the self is not fully individuated or unified as it is purported to be in the West, but is thought to be familial and communal, defining itself foremost as part of a close-knit group. However, even in these societies, the self is not entirely communal or cohesive. Indeed, there exists a contradiction between an outer shell or public self and an inner core or private self, both of which are integral to the overall sense of the self. Psychologically, the core is supposed to be private, stable, intimate and reliable, while the exterior is construed to be unstable and unreliable, the domain of surfaces, corruption and worldly influences.[4] The self's duality necessitates a boundary zone, which like a veil or a screen can protect the core from contamination from the outside and, acting similar to 'screen memory',[5] it can prevent the core from leaking to the outside.

Modesty as Social Practice

Iranian social hermeneutics are driven by these dynamic and artful strategies, which are essentially based on distrusting manifest meanings and concealing and protecting core values. People are thus motivated to search for hidden, inner meanings in all they see, hear and receive in daily interaction with others, while trying to conceal their own intentions. Since women are taken to be a constitutive part of the male core self, they must be protected from the vision of unrelated

males by following a set of rules of modesty which apply to architecture, dress, behaviour, voice, eye contact and relationships. Walls, words and veils mark, mask, separate and confine both women and men.[6] Instances abound in Iranian culture: high walls separate and conceal private space from public space; the inner rooms of a house protect/hide the family; the veil hides women; formal language suppresses unbridled public expression of private feelings; modesty suppresses and conceals women; decorum and status hide men; the exoteric meanings of religious texts hide the esoteric meanings; and perspectiveless miniature paintings convey their messages in layers instead of presenting a unified and clear vision for a centred viewer. In Iranian cinema, modesty necessitates that men and women treat each other at all times as though they are in public, even when they are in the privacy of their own home or bedroom. The repercussions of this on the diegetic characters' behaviour, dress, voice and gaze, and on the film's capacity for realistic representation of women are explored later.

Veiling is the armature of modesty, requiring further elaboration. With the onset of menstruation girls must cover their hair, body parts and body shape by wearing either a veil, a chador or some other modest garb, including headscarf, loose tunic, and long trousers. They need not cover themselves from all men, but only from those who are unrelated (*namahram*) to them. Women's husbands, sons, brothers, fathers and uncles are considered to be related (*mahram*); before them, they need not wear the veil, but they are still required to be modest. On the other hand, women must veil themselves in the presence of unrelated men and unrelated men must avert their eyes.

In the aesthetics of veiling, the voice has a complementary function. Before entering a house, men are required to make their presence known by voice in order to give the women inside a chance to cover themselves or to organise the scene for the male gaze. Women must not only veil their bodies from unrelated men but also to some extent their voice. Veiling of the voice includes using formal language with unrelated males and females, a decorous tone of voice and avoiding singing, boisterous laughter and any emotional outburst in public other than expression of grief or anger.

However, veiling as a social practice is not fixed or unidirectional; instead, it is a dynamic practice in which both men and women are implicated. In addition, there is a dialectical relationship between veiling and unveiling: that which covers is also capable of uncovering. In practice, women have a great deal of latitude in how they present themselves to the gaze of the male onlookers, involving body language, eye contact, type of veil, clothing worn underneath the veil and the manner in which the veil itself is fanned open or closed at strategic moments to lure or to mask, to reveal or to conceal the face, the body, or the clothing underneath. Shahla Haeri aptly notes the dynamic relationship that exists between veiling and vision:

> [N]ot only does the veil deny the penetrating male gaze, it enables women to use their own judiciously. Because men and women are forbidden to socialize with each other, or to come into contact, their gazes find new dimensions in Muslim Iran. Not easily controllable, or subject to religious curfew, glances become one of the most intricate and locally meaningful means of communication between the genders.[7]

This 'communication' involves not only voyeurism and exhibitionism but also a system of surveillance – a system of controlling the look and of being controlled by the look. Veiling, therefore, is not a panoptic process in the manner Foucault[8] describes because vision is not in the possession of only one side; both women and men organise the field of vision of the other.

Umm Kalthoum, after 1945. Postcard. Courtesy of Sarah Graham-Brown. Following an early career as a singer of religious songs, Kalthoum went on to become an Arab diva whose love songs were full of passion and sexual tension.

Modesty and the System of Looking

The constitution of the self as dual means that a series of veils, screens, and distances are posited – between inside and outside, self and other, and women and men. Additionally, since the construction of the self as familial and communal is not total or hermetic, there is always a distance, screen, or veil between individual sovereignty and group solidarity. These and other forms of duality and distantiation create both ambivalence about and a desire for unity through reunion of subject and object, with profound repercussions for vision, hearing, and cinema.

Distance and veiling are constitutive components of pleasure derived from looking. Freud posited scopophilia (pleasure in looking at another as an object of sexual stimulation) as a libidinal drive that works through both pleasure and unpleasure. In its pleasurable aspect, scopophilia demands a distance between subject and object because 'it is in the play of absence and distance that desire is activated'.[9] Modesty and the system of looking which has developed to deal with modesty veil aspects of women (and to some extent of men) and thereby create the necessary distance that motivates and promotes pleasurable looking as well as listening. They also tend to turn the objects of the look into eroticised subjects. Veiled women thus may become highly charged with sexuality, which ironically subverts the purpose of the religious principles of veiling, which is to protect women from becoming sexual objects. A person draws pleasure from listening to or viewing a scene to which he/she is not supposed to be privy. To be sure, walls and veils segregate people but they do not isolate them completely. Indeed, they tend to invite curiosity and afford pleasure through voyeurism, eavesdropping and exhibitionism. Overtly repressive, veiling promotes not only voyeurism and its obverse, exhibitionism (unveiling), but also a culture of surveillance. These effects of veiling are inflected in classical Iranian miniature paintings in which figures are invariably shown inside homes, palaces and gardens, peering at or listening to others from behind windows, curtains, doors and bushes.

The 'Islamic' Averted Look

The psychology and ideology of a dual self and of modesty tend to produce a unique system of looking that is based on masochistic pleasure. Major Shi'ite religious scholars (*mujtaheds*), such as the Ayatollah Ruhollah Khomeini[10] and Ayatollah Sayyed Abolqasem Musavi Kho'i,[11] have developed or affirmed existing commandments for looking (*ahkam-e negah kardan*). These commandments, for example, forbid males or females from looking, with or without lust, at bare bodies or body parts of people of the opposite sex to whom they are unrelated. Males are forbidden to look at women's hair and women are obliged to cover it. Looking at sexual organs of others is forbidden whether it is done directly, through a glass, in a mirror, reflected in water or, by extension, in films.[12]

In reality, of course, men and women do look at each other with desire and lust, but to satisfy the rules of modesty, a situationist grammar of looking has evolved that ranges from the direct but guilty gaze to what I have called the averted look. In the latter case, people avoid looking at others directly, based on differences such as those of class, hierarchy and gender. When meeting each other, people tend to either look down or look at the other's face in an unfocused way so as to avoid definitive eye contact.[13] On the other hand, someone who is not looking, or a stranger (an unrelated person), is scrutinised with a direct gaze until they notice they are being watched; at that point, the looker averts his eyes guiltily. This play between the averted and direct gaze is partially responsible for the contradictory impression by outsiders that Iranians are both evasive and aggressive.

Rakhshan Banietemad, *Nargess*, 1991. Film still. Film produced by Arman Film. Here, direct eye contact is avoided between the sexes.

At first glance, the averted look appears to be the opposite of Zizek's 'looking awry' that, according to him, makes things clearer than the direct gaze because it is charged with (and distorted by) the desires and anxieties of the looker.[14] On closer examination, however, the averted look proves to be anamorphic like the awry look because, on the one hand, it is charged with the voyeuristic and masochistic desires of the looker and, on the other, it inscribes the codes of modesty. This produces understandings between lookers and objects of the look which are clearer than those obtainable through the unveiled direct gaze.

Inscribing Averted Look and Direct Gaze in Cinema

Cinema created a serious ideological crisis for the Islamic Republic, for it threatened to break down or seriously problematise the prevailing Islamic barriers of gender segregation, modesty and veiling during film production (on the set), during exhibition (on the screen) and during reception (in cinemas). In all these situations, unrelated women and men have to work together in situations of intimacy and professionalism – producing films; appearing on screen together; and watching films together as cinema audiences. Cinema posed an additional threat because its stories made the private and intimate lives of its subjects public, therein countering the whole ideology and practice of modesty and veiling. Here, I will concentrate my analysis primarily on the way rules of modesty were manipulated, resisted and inscribed in films.

Although veiling, modesty, the direct gaze and the averted look existed, to various degrees, in cinema under Shah Mohammad Reza Pahlavi, they were first codified in cinema only after the revolution, in 1982.[15] However, these systems of looking did not remain static; instead, they developed steadily towards liberal and counterhegemonic interpretations. The evolution

of the codes and the increasing involvement of women both behind and in front of the cameras occurred in three overlapping phases.

Phase I: Absence (early 1980s)

During the first phase, immediately after the revolution, images of unveiled women were cut from existing Iranian and imported films. When cutting caused unacceptable narrative confusion – and it did, as some films were cut by over half an hour – the offending parts were blacked out directly in the frames with magic markers. As part of the purification process which occurred in this phase, all existing films were reviewed and the majority were banned. For example, of 2,208 locally made films that were reviewed, only 252 received exhibition permits.

Women were generally excised from new local productions through self-censorship by a frightened industry unsure of official attitudes and regulations regarding cinema. Instead, many film-makers resorted to making war films and children's films (or adult films that involved children) – two new genres of post-revolutionary cinema. As a result, the cinema of this phase was primarily patriarchal and male-centred. Because the direct gaze of desire was unofficially prohibited after the revolution, the averted, unfocused look became predominant in film but in a highly complex manner which evolved over the years.

Phase II: Pale Presence (mid-1980s)

In this phase, women appeared in local productions either as ghostly presences in the background or as domesticated subjects in the home. They were rarely the bearers of the story or the plot. An aesthetics and grammar of vision and veiling based on gender segregation developed, which governed the characters' location, dress, posture, behaviour, voice and gaze.

Female characters were often confined to the home and wore a headscarf, chador or veil, and a long, loose-fitting tunic. They behaved in a dignified manner and avoided body contact of any sort with men, even if they were related to them by marriage or by birth. As a prominent actress in exile, who had worked in the early years of the Islamic Republic, told me in an interview, actors and actresses were forbidden from touching each other or from establishing direct or desirous eye contact on screen, making realistic acting very difficult. Such professional difficulties were in part responsible for her decision to go into exile in the United States.[16] The evolving filming grammar also discouraged close-up photography of women's faces or exchanges of desirous looks between men and women. In fact, cinematic looking, which in the Pahlavi era was often direct and highly charged with sexuality, was desexualised and replaced by the averted look. In addition, women were usually filmed in long and medium shots and were shown in inactive roles to prevent the contours of their bodies from showing. As a result of these aversive strategies, both women and men were desexualised and cinematic texts became androgynous. Dariush Mehrjui, a well-known male director who has made a series of films about women (bearing the protagonists' names as titles) encapsulated the situation when he told me in an interview: 'In post-revolutionary cinema the religiously unlawful (*haram*) look does not exist. All women must be treated like one's own sister.'[17] Love and the physical expression of love (even between intimates) were also absent.

These strategies of veiling and aversion tended to subvert the system of suture (the symbolic insertion of spectators into the film's story) based on point-of-view shots and on the direct (unveiled) relay of the gazes between characters in shot reverse-shot situations. The unfocused look, the averted look, the fleeting glance, the desexualised look and the long shot – all instances of inscription of modesty in cinema – problematise Western cinematic theories, which rely on audience implication through suturing, because they impede audience identification with characters on the screen. These are factors that are ignored by scholars whose writings on the veil in cinema are based solely on the application of Western feminist theories, disregarding the complexity of the social situation of veiling and of the ramifications of the indigenous theories of both the gaze and of spectatorship.

In the classical Hollywood cinema style, the spectator is made 'invisible' through various strategies of mise-en-scène, shot composition and continuity editing which do not acknowledge the presence of the spectators – thus turning them into voyeurs.[18] However, the spectators are not just subjects of the film texts and their relationship to the film is not merely textual or psychological but also social. The rules of modesty and veiling, therefore, impact not only upon the poetics of Iranian films but also upon the politics of the films' reception by spectators. Spectators are considered to be structurally unrelated to the persons projected on the screen and thus must be treated as if they were present at the time of filming. This necessitates that women and men within the diegesis observe the rules of modesty and codes of dress, gaze, voice and behaviour in relationship not only to each other but also to the spectators. As unrelated persons, spectators cannot be privy to unveiled women on the screen or to intimate moments between them and their male counterparts, involving exchanges of amorous gazes and erotic contacts (touching, hugging, or kissing). This forces the actors playing the parts of husband and wife in the privacy of their bedroom, for example, to behave as though they were not alone and not related. Thus, in Iranian cinema the spectator is encoded in the film's diegesis by strategies of editing and suture and is inscribed in the profilmic situation by Islamic codes of modesty. While the former is designed to make invisible the machination of ideology, the latter is calculated to make it manifest. This unusual and contradictory situation presents a real dilemma for directors and actors, male and female.

In this phase, one of the most significant consequences of inscribing modesty and spectators in the films was that film-makers were forced to represent all spaces as if they were public. This resulted in unrealistic and distorted representation of women, since they were shown veiling themselves from their next of kin and in the privacy of their homes – something they would not do in real life. This was true even if the diegetic husband and wife were married to each other in real life. This undermined the voyeuristic structure of looking that Western film theorists posited for cinema, which is based on the unawareness of the subject that she is being watched. Another result was that non-verbal intimacy was effaced from the screen for quite some time, as women veiled not only their bodies but also their sentiments. This tended to present a formidable challenge to the actors who had to express their feelings to their intimate relatives in psychologically realistic ways, without gazing into their eyes or touching them.[19] Poetry became the only option for expressing intimacy, at first primarily for the men. Another result of veiling was that certain historical periods (such as the pre-revolution era) and certain civilizations (such as the West) were closed to Iranian cinema, because of the unrepresentability of the unveiled women in those periods and civilisations.

Many of these points can be illustrated by examining the early feature films of the foremost Iranian woman director, Rakhshan Banietemad. Her *Kharej az Mahdudeh* (*Off the Limit*, 1987) is about a young middle-class couple in Tehran who discover that their newly acquired house is located in a district that has accidentally been omitted from the city zoning maps and that, to all intents and purposes, does not exist and is not subject to the jurisdiction and protection of any legal or police authority. As a result, thieves and robbers have a field day in this no-man's-land known as Chaos City (*hertabad*). The residents are placed off limit, out of bounds, and therefore made invisible (veiled). However, in a move towards self-determination (visibility), they begin to enforce the laws themselves, capturing the thieves and reforming them. As a result, the city's name changes to New City (*nowabad*). The film is a biting social satire that criticises the chaotic post-1979 social conditions, but to avoid the post-revolutionary censors, it conveniently labels it as belonging to 1972. Despite this criticism, Banietemad reproduces the dominant view of women under the Islamic Republic, for the wife is uncritically so confined to the home that her husband must do the shopping for their daily necessities. Moreover, the wife is deprived of the one avenue of intimate expression available to women, recitation of poetry. Her husband, however, has access to it, as in a scene in which he recites a famous love ballad to her while she serves him his meal. This is clearly a phase-II representation of women. American and Iranian audiences abroad have expressed surprise that the director of such a traditional representation of women was a woman. Despite its timidity in representing the wife, the film is somewhat bold in the political solution that it offers to the community's dilemma. For it urges the community to take charge, restore order and patrol its own boundaries. Ultimately, however, the zealotry of this new order is no less problematic than the lawlessness of the previous order.

The aesthetics of veiling, which govern the actors' behaviour, dress and emotional expression, also affect *Kharej az Mahdudeh*'s mise-en-scène and filming style. Objects and boundary-marking features such as fences, walls and columns constantly obstruct vision. Long tracking shots with these obstacles in the foreground highlight them as visual barriers and as metaphors for modesty and veiling. The reciprocity of veiling and unveiling, however, necessitates that the obstructions which seem to *conceal* certain things from view also *reveal* something else, namely, the director's intention. Indeed, in one of the early shots, before the residents of Chaos City have realised their zoning problem, the camera looks down from above the walls of a house into the adjacent street. In the background, the husband is walking down the street, alongside a wall. In the foreground, a fence made of barbed wire and dry bushes on top of the wall partially obstructs the view of the street below. Towards the film's end, after the community has taken up the enforcement of the laws, a similarly composed shot is shown, but with a major difference. The foreground is no longer a decrepit fence but a row of beautiful flowers in full bloom, signalling the transformation from Chaos City to New City. The director's activist vision – that beauty and prosperity require political will and independent action – is made visible in the barrier that conceals vision. That which veils also unveils.

In her next film *Zard-e Qanari* (*Canary Yellow*, 1989), Banietemad depicts the women of a family, particularly the mother, to be strong, mature, level-headed and ruling the men, who are presented as naïve and unscrupulous. Despite this, the film's central moral character is a man, who defiantly demonstrates that virtue overpowers vice. This ambivalent configuration of female/male power relations points to the internal tension between liberalism and conservatism both in Banietemad's works and in Iranian society as a whole.

The politics and poetics of veiling also affected the on-screen relationship of the men in phase II, resulting in fascinating gender and sexual reconfigurations that were sometimes inimical to the ruling ideology, such as those that suggested male homoeroticism, a form of sexuality that is severely punished in Islamic Iran. In Mohammad Reza A'lami's *Noqteh Za'f* (*The Weak Point*, 1983), the relationship between a political activist and the security agent who captures him displays strong but ambiguous homoeroticism and gender crossover. The two men interact as though the captive were a woman. They engage in activities that are shown typically in boy-meets-girl-and-falls-in-love films. Playing soccer in the park, they pass the ball back and forth like two lovers and, at the beach, seated side by side, they gaze at the horizon while a wild horse gallops by as extradiegetic romantic music seals the moment.

The incorporation of modesty in films, which discouraged emotional expression and intimacy between men and women, had another interesting consequence for interpreting scenes that were filmed in the somewhat relaxed phase-II style. For example, mere close-ups of women or two-shots showing a man and a woman alone together engaged in simple conversation, could be interpreted by the spectators as intimate love scenes, even though the contents of the shot were not in any way explicit. In this manner, an 'innocent' shot could become charged with intimacy and sexuality. Such examples demonstrate that in order to understand the significance and evolution of representation of women in cinema, codes and texts as well as meanings and contexts must be examined.

Phase III: Powerful Presence (since the late 1980s)

This phase appeared gradually and was marked by the more dramatic presence of women both on the screen in strong leading roles and behind the cameras as directors. A 1991 film entitled *Beh Khater-e Hameh Chiz* (*For Everything*), directed by Rajab Mohammadin, is an example of the changed screen presence of women. It examines with moving realism the difficult lives of garment workers, *all* of whom are women – a far cry from an all-male cast just a few years earlier in phase I. As the director comments: 'Previously [during the Pahlavi regime], Iranian women were portrayed as miserable, ignorant and superficial creatures who

were used by men for sexual or decorative purposes. I wanted to tell a story in which women were virtuous, active, and socially constructive.'[20]

While laudable, this replacement of the negative images of women by wholly positive ones does not guarantee a more realistic and complex representation. The accomplishment was not counterhegemonic in so far as it replicated the dominant/subordinate relations of power between men and women in the society at large. The ways of seeing which the dominant patriarchal and Islamic ethos engendered in Iran was complex and contradictory: at the same time that it oppressed women, it empowered them.

The strong presence of women behind the camera was officially recognised in 1990, when the Ninth Fajr Film Festival – Iran's foremost film event – devoted a whole programme to women's cinema. This cinema is now very diverse, as women are involved in all aspects of feature, documentary, short subject and animated films, as well as in all aspects of television films and serials production. Some of the film-makers are quite versatile and make documentaries, television soap operas and feature films; their output has been abundant. More importantly, almost all of the women directors named in note 2 have directed several films, demonstrating that after the purification process (phase I) and the institutionalisation of the veil (phase II), film-making became, not a one-off shot-in-the-dark, but a legitimate profession for women (phase III). Increase in quantity, however, has not been matched by corresponding improvement in quality, which remains uneven. It would be politically naïve to expect that women directors in the Islamic Republic necessarily present a more rounded or a more radically feminist perspective in their films than the male directors. In fact, particularly during phases I and II, many of them did not (Banietemad's phase-II films are cases in point); however, since phase III, the situation has gradually improved with the liberalisation of modesty rules.[21]

Rakhshan Banietemad, *Nargess*, 1991. Film still. Film produced by Arman Film. The women's defiant gaze directly at the camera would have been inconceivable only a few years earlier in Iranian cinema.

To examine in more detail the dynamics of the evolution of the rules of modesty in cinema across the three phases, the remainder of this essay is devoted to the emergence of a single theme – love.

Love Finds a Way

From the mid-1980s onwards, film-makers took tentative steps to question, and even to subvert, the averted look, rules of modesty, asexual behaviour and gendered spatiality, creating a fluid cinematic atmosphere and an increasing number of transgressive films. For example, the theme of love, which was almost absent from films in the first two phases because of restrictions on dress, looking, touching, acting, voicing and filming, began to be explored with increasing boldness. As expected, however, this proved to be a sensitive subject, fraught with anxiety, contentiousness and uncertainty.

Such sensitivity towards the hitherto taboo subject of love resulted in either the film-maker's use of children as substitutes for women; in the metaphoric treatment of love; in using mediating erotic objects between the sexes; or in official censorship if the approach to the subject was bold and open. An early and daring example that used more than one of these strategies was Bahram Baizai's engrossing pacifist film *Bashu, Gharibeh-ye Kuchak* (*Bashu, the Little Stranger*, 1985). The narrative fabric is interwoven with the textured relationship of Nai, a single mother, and Bashu, a boy escaping the Iraqi attacks during the Iraq-Iran war. Women have always played a central role as narrative agents in Baizai's films and, in *Bashu, Gharibeh-ye Kuchak*, Nai occupies such a position. In the absence of her husband, who is at the war front, she works the fields, takes care of her children and, in accepting the dislocated boy, defies tradition and the authority of her family and village elders. What adds to the enrichment of the relationship between Nai and Bashu is the

150 Veil

ambiguous position of Bashu both as a boy whom Nai takes care of and protects and as a man she nurtures and loves and on whom she depends. When her children first warn her of the presence of Bashu the stranger among the bushes, Nai is off camera and the film cuts to a shot showing empty space. Suddenly, Nai rises into the frame in a surprising close-up, her hair and chin covered with a white scarf, emphasising her dramatic and intense eyes. With a single shot that draws attention to the alluring possibilities of unveiled vision, direct gaze, and scopophilia, Baizai breaks years of entrapment by rules of modesty. Gazing directly into the camera in close-up, Nai visually addresses both the spectators and Bashu hiding in the bushes. This shot conflates their points of view, resulting in both the spectators and Bashu becoming subjects of Nai's gaze, just as Nai is the subject of theirs. In this way, Bashu becomes a substitute for the spectators: men identify with him as a man vis-à-vis Nai and women see him as a surrogate son or brother. This ambiguity turns him into a dual vehicle, sending and receiving both love and compassion. Finally, the direct relay of looks between the characters in *Bashu, Gharibeh-ye Kuchak* positions the spectators as related to the characters, thereby ensuring their suture into the diegesis. Here Baizai clearly favours unveiling but, working within the confines of a modesty-driven society, love and gaze enter his film only intricately and ambiguously.

That the film's release was delayed for several years may have less to do with its implicit antiwar message (which is the usual reason given) than with its bold transgression of codes of modesty and spectator positioning. As Baizai told me in an interview, the censors demanded that he make some eighty changes to the film, including removing the close-up face shot just discussed. He refused to do so until the political climate had sufficiently changed, when the film was finally released to great public response and without many of the demanded elisions.[22]

Bahram Baizai, *Bashu, Gharibeh-ye Kuchak*, 1985. Film still. Film distributed by International Home Cinema.

The shift towards a bolder treatment of love and transgressive looking gradually took root, but in fits and starts. Several films in the early 1990s transgressed the semiotics of the averted look and the aesthetics of vision and veiling, with positive results. For instance, Mehrdad Fakhimi's film *Arus* (*Bride*, 1991), about the love of a newly-wed couple, utilises close-up photography of the bride's face and the direct gaze in ways that border on fetishistic scopophilia. However, the film escaped a ban and was widely exhibited, garnering the highest box office record in the history of Iranian cinema to date. The switch in this film from the averted glance to the direct gaze may have been one significant reason for its popularity with audiences and the popular press.

Film-makers resorted to a variety of ingenuous substitutes, third parties, doubles, objects, or even animals that mediated between the principals, passing on their desires and charged intimacy. In Mohsen Makhmalbaf's *Gabbeh* (1985), for example, in a long shot, we see Gabbeh seated behind the goat and milking it vigorously, as her suitor approaches and positions himself in front of the goat. He then looks at Gabbeh and clearly establishes eye contact with her and begins to gently caress the goat's horns. Then, in a close-up we see her looking up at him as her hands move to and fro. In another close-up, he is seen standing, looking at her with pleasure and reciting poetry to her. The suggestion of intimacy, even fellatio, is clear, but the two principals never touch each other. In a scene in Ebrahim Hatamikia's *Az Karkheh ta Rhine* (*From Karkheh to Rhine*, 1992), where an injured war veteran has to hug his sister, a male double is used for the sister and the scene is filmed in long shot, with the double's back to the audience. In the final scene of Banietemad's *Nargess* (1991), a struggle between a thief named Adel and his young wife Nargess over love and money is staged so that they wrestle with the bag of money that is between them, without ever touching each other. Likewise in Banietemad's *Banu-ye Ordibehesht* (*The May Lady*, 1997), a concerned single mother named Forugh comforts her rebellious teenage son and expresses her love by means of mediating objects: in one scene, a towel with which she dries his wet hair, and in another, a blanket through which she caresses him.

Banu-ye Ordibehesht pushes the boundaries of modesty and averted looking further by centring the story on a female documentary film-maker who is a divorced single mother insisting on pursuing her profession, on her liaison with a man to whom she is not married, and on her raising of her rebellious teenage boy. However, the film breaks more than just the thematic taboos of divorce, single motherhood and unmarried relations with men. It also expands the vocabulary of veiling, voicing and modesty by introducing fascinating textual and narrative innovations – forced by the imposition of the veil.

One of these textual innovations is the way mise-en-scène and filming suggest unveiling. In one shot, the diegetic director Forugh arrives home from a day's hard work filming a documentary. In a medium shot, she walks through a hallway towards her bedroom. The camera pans with her as she walks briskly in that direction. As she gets close to the door, she reaches for her headscarf and lifts it in a characteristic gesture that signals the imminent removal of the scarf. But just before the scarf is off, she disappears through the door, leaving the unmistakable impression of unveiling without actually having done it. Unlike some male directors, such as Dariush Mehrjui in his *Leila* (1997), who have attempted by means of clever mise-en-scène and filming to either deny the existence of the veil or to distract the audience from the artificiality of the veil in private spaces, Banietemad ingeniously incorporates it in *Banu-ye Ordibehesht* as a natural part of the diegesis. As Norma Claire Moruzzi observes, this direct incorporation of veiling as 'a cinematic issue may be the most effective way of establishing the film's realism'.[23] The result is intensified spectator identification with diegetic characters.

One of the narrative innovations in this film is the way the male lover is simultaneously both effaced and inscribed by means of a complex game of veiling and unveiling, as well as voicing and unvoicing. He is visually absent from the entire film, but is simultaneously present throughout by means of telephone, letters and voiceover poetry. Using her cordless telephone, Forugh talks with him frequently and intimately. They also exchange letters and – using one of the favourite Iranian devices of intimacy, sexuality and love – quote poetry to each other. While throughout these exchanges the woman is the primary speaking subject, from time to time, the man's voice is heard on the phone or reading his own poetic and flowery letters to her. In addition, Forugh's voice on the soundtrack tells of her feelings and thoughts about her son, her career, her films and her lover, deepening our access to her subjectivity. The lovers' voices on the soundtrack reading letters and poems to each other and Forugh's autobiographical voiceover musings create a dense tapestry of free indirect discourse braided together by various voices and subjectivities. This is the first example of this discourse that I know of in an Iranian feature film.

These interweaving male and female voices symbolically substitute for the desired but dreaded – because outlawed – physical contact between unmarried couples. By means of verbal and epistolary communication, the protagonists are able to express their mutual love for one another and by means of voice fusion, they are able to become one, vocally. None of this expression would have been possible if the characters were shown together. This is because veiling rules do not govern vision and voice uniformly. By cleverly taking advantage of this discrepancy, voice contact more than replaces the missing eye contact between the lovers which would have been constrained anyway, or would have been deflected and averted by unfulfilled desire and by modesty rules.

During phase III, despite the continued oppression of women and draconian censorship, the constraints on women's representation lessened and film-makers pushed the boundaries of what was allowed with each film, not only dealing with taboo subjects, such as love and passion, but also expressing those themes in aesthetically counterhegemonic ways. Not all women directors abided fully or equally by the regulations. Some fought them by indirection, implication and aversion, such as the early Banietemad. Others, such as Tahmineh Milani, faced them head-on. Some women, who began conservatively, like Banietemad and Puran Derakhshandeh, became bolder with each film. A younger generation of women directors, such as Samira Makhmalbaf and Marziyeh Meshkini, who grew up in more open times, began their careers with stronger representations of women, flouting the veiling rules. Moreover, women were not alone in these representational struggles, as several prominent male directors, such as Baizai, Mehrjui and Mohsen Makhmalbaf, engaged in sustained efforts of both sorts. While all women directors cast women in key roles, not all the male directors did so, even the films of a director as prominent as Abbas Kiarostami lacked a significant female presence until his 2002 film *Dah* (*Ten*). While women's presence as directors is impressive, they are highly underrepresented in many technical and business areas of the film industry, such as in cinematography and film distribution and exhibition.

Finally, a large number of Iranian women directors work in exile and diaspora in Europe and North America in all formats and genres of film, television and video. As might be expected, deterritorialisation and immigration destabilised the traditional Iranian patriarchy, bringing prominence to women's social and political status and to the questioning of gender relations, a prominence that was inscribed in the form of strong women protagonists who subverted authoritarian relations. The increasing screen presence of women may also be due to their increasing presence behind the cameras. In a recent study, I discovered that 21% of Iranian directors of all films types working in Europe and North America were women (44 out of 210 directors), with the largest percentage (40%) working in the United States, the site of the largest Iranian population in diaspora.[24] While this female/male director ratio appears to be small, it is probably much higher than it was in Iran when the 1979 revolution drove many Iranians into exile. Among the most accomplished, innovative, or prolific women film-makers who have worked outside Iran are Shirin Bazleh (USA), Shirin Estessam (USA), Farideh Fardjam (the Netherlands), Ghazel Radpay (France/Iran), Marva Nabili (USA), Shirin Neshat (USA), Soudabeh Oskoui-Babcock (USA), Mitra Tabrizian (UK), Persheng Sadegh Vaziri (USA/Iran) and Mehrnaz Saeed Vafa (USA). Interestingly, a few of them returned home to Iran to make films there and a few who normally work at home made films abroad for home consumption. This crossing of geographical and national boundaries – which is also occurring with male film-makers – is part of the globalisation of Iranian cinema and of cinema in general, which has led to the emergence of a new worldwide cinematic formation, which I have called 'accented cinema'.[25] A great majority of female accented cinéastes work in the genres of short and non-theatrical film, which are generally more receptive to women, minority and alternative artists. Significantly, even though they are outside the reach of Islamic Iran, the iconography, poetics and power relations of the veil continue to capture the imagination of these film-makers, something particularly evident in the video installations of Shirin Neshat[26] and Ghazel.[27]

Mitra Tabrizian, *Surveillance*, 1990. Photograph, 300cm x 120cm. Text: Homi K. Bhabha; lighting: Andy Golding; set: Richard Rudnicki; costume: Behyat Rezaei; production: Zadoc Nava, David Carpenter. Cast: Steve Brooks, James Donald, Gair Dunlop, Souad Faress, Rod Gill, Merlin John, Sian Martin, Orson Nava, Robert Peck, Zim Percival, Eitan, Kaveh, Nader, Tower. The project was partly funded by the Photographers' Gallery, London.

In His name
memory is mute.
History speaks
in the quickening
of the dead.

When I was 11, I won the big cup in ice-skating
(at Ghasre-Yakh). My parents weren't there
to take any pictures. My brother and my best friend
and my other friend didn't speak a word to me
for days. They said that the club-owner's son
was probably in love with me and that's why i
had won. But the others said that I was really
good. i came home with my big cup,
which is still standing all dusty in the basement.

Ghazel, *Me I*, 1997–98. Video,
24 mins.

gotta be a feminist

Ghazel, *Me* series, 2002. Video.

promise that i'll be a good scarecrow

Ghazel, *Me* series, 2002. Video.

Since Ghazel's works are featured in the *Veil* exhibition, it is worth mentioning a few words about her *Me* series. The series constitutes some forty planned short films, collectively lasting nearly eight hours. Each film is between ten to twelve minutes and contains ten autonomous scenes – each presenting a single shot of Ghazel herself engaged in some activity – bringing her total output to an astonishingly high four hundred individual scenes. In this manner, multiplication, repetition, and fragmentation – characteristics of accented cinema – are inscribed at a structural level in her films. Ironically, however, their contents bear a strong cohesive and single-minded preoccupation, even obsessiveness, with a few overarching ideas: the film-maker's biography, the black chador which she wears in all the scenes and the contradictory position of women under the Islamic Republic.

Like many Iranian artists, cartoonists and film-makers, particularly those working abroad, Ghazel's *Me* films turn the veil into an agent by which to critique and mock the Islamic Republic and demonstrate the incompatibility of the veil with modernity. However, Ghazel does so in a more nuanced manner. On the one hand, the veil tends to exoticise and homogenise women in her films, robbing them of their individuality, subjectivity and personality, given that the protagonist is never explicitly identified as a real person with a history, story, or point of view. In this sense, the veil functions more as a semiotic placeholder for women than as a realistic representation of women. On the other hand, the woman in the *Me* films is physically active, continually concocting schemes, performing tasks and displaying herself for the camera. Indeed, nothing, not even the tightly worn veil, seems to deter her from honing her skills and playing around. In this manner, she takes the discourse of the veil away from the official culture and from its stalwart critics by actively and personally demonstrating that,

while veiled, women can have fun and can learn to ski downhill, water-ski or ice-skate. Equally, veiled women can want to drive motorcycles, swim, stay in good physical shape, or become Miss Universe; they can also be critical of the housing problems, food shortages, war conditions and the detentions and executions that have beset Iran. Most artists and film-makers do not deal with such activities or find them incompatible with the veil, which they mock with their juxtapositions of incongruous worlds. Although Ghazel's films also partake of this mocking attitude, they also contain genuine humour that is not condescending either to their female diegetic subject and spectators, or to Muslim women in general. As a result, her viewers do not so much laugh *at* the diegetic woman (or at veiled women in general) as they laugh *with* her at the incongruities of her life. Because Ghazel is autobiographically implicated in the films, because the protagonist is an active woman rather than a politicised or aestheticised sign system, and because the veil does not totally represent, subjugate, or define the woman, Ghazel's films widen the rather narrowly defined discourse of the veil. Her juxtapositions of the veil are also not metaphorical or abstract, but are based on its real presence in women's lives and on the paradoxes that it creates. The expression of veiling is thus unveiled and direct.

This essay is a considerably revised version of two articles: 'Veiled Visions/Powerful Presences: Women in Postrevolutionary Iranian Cinema', in *In the Eye of the Storm: Women in Postrevolutionary Iran*, edited by Mahnaz Afkhami and Erika Friedl, London and New York: I.B. Tauris and Syracuse University Press, 1994, pp. 131–50; and 'Veiled Voice and Vision in Iranian Cinema: the Evolution of Rakhshan Banietemad's Films', in *Ladies and Gentlemen, Boys and Girls: Gender in Film at the End of the 20th Century*, edited by Murray Pomerance, New York: State University of New York Press, 2001, pp. 36–53.

Notes

1. Rosen, Miriam. 'The Camera Art: an Interview with Abbas Kiarostami,' *cinéaste* 19: 2–3, 1992, p. 40.

2. They are: Tahmineh Ardekani (died in a plane crash in 1995), Faryal Behzad, Rakhshan Banietemad, Marziyeh Borumand, Puran Derakhshandeh, Zohreh Mahasti Badii, Samira Makhmalbaf, Yasmin Maleknasr, Marziyeh Meshkini, Tahmineh Milani, Kobra Saidi and Maryam Shahriar.

3. See Naficy, 'Iranian Cinema', in *Companion Encyclopedia of Middle Eastern and North African Film*, edited by Oliver Leaman, London: Routledge, 2001, pp. 130–222; and Naficy, 'Islamizing Film Culture in Iran', in *Iran: Political Culture in the Islamic Republic*, edited by Samih Farsoun and Mehrdad Mashayekhi, London: Routledge and Kegan Paul, 1992, pp. 173–208.

4. Beeman, William. *Language, Status, and Power in Iran*. Bloomington: Indiana University Press, 1986.

5. Freud, Sigmund. *The Standard Edition of the Complete Works of Sigmund Freud*, translated by James Strachy, London, 1953–73, vol. III, p. 307)

6. Milani, Farzaneh. *Veils and Words: The Emerging Voice of Iranian Women Writers*. Syracuse: Syracuse University Press, 1992.

7. Haeri, Shahla. *Law of Desire: Temporary Marriage in Shi'i Iran*, Syracuse: Syracuse University Press, 1989, p. 229.

8. Foucault, Michel. *Discipline and Punish: The Birth of the Prison*, translated by Alan Sheridan, New York: Vantage, 1979.

9. Kuhn, Annette. *Women's Pictures: Feminism and Cinema*. New York: Routledge and Kegan Paul, 1982, p. 58.

10. Khomeini, Ruhollah. *Towzihol Masa'el (ba Ezafat va Masa'el-e Jadid)*, no place of publication, n.d.

11. Kho'i, Sayyed Abolqasem Musavi. *Resaleh-ye Towzih-al Masa'el*, no place of publication: Entesharat-e Javidan, 1975/1395.

12. On the subject of photography there are divergent opinions. For example, Khomeini states that it was not forbidden for a man to take pictures of an unrelated woman, while Kho'i declares that a man is forbidden not only from taking pictures of an unrelated woman but also from looking at her picture if he knows her. As a young boy, for example, the older women in my family would either not permit me to take their picture or would only let me do so if they were covered by their veil. Their reason was that although I was related to them, the men developing the photographs were not. I had to engage in a game of veiling and unveiling with them by either pretending that I was not taking their pictures (while I actually was) or snapping their pictures when they were not aware.

13. This behaviour of averting one's gaze fits the tenets of the Quran, which warns Muslims against the danger of the direct gaze.

14. Zizek, Slavoj. 'Looking Awry', in *October*, no. 51, 1990, p. 34.

15. For a full discussion, see Naficy, 'Iranian Cinema', op. cit.

16 Naficy, interview with Iranian actress who wishes to remain anonymous, Los Angeles, April 1988.

17. Naficy, interview with Dariush Mehrjui, Los Angeles, April 1990.

18. Metz, Christian. *The Imaginary Signifier: Psychoanalysis and the Cinema*, Bloomington: Indiana University Press, 1982.

19. Naficy, 'Zan va Mas'aleh-ye Zan dar Sinema-ye Iran-e Ba'd az Enqelab,' in *Nimeye Digar* 14, Spring 1991, pp. 123–69.

20. 'For the Sake of Women's Image', in *Mahnameh-ye Sinema' i-ye Film*, no. 117, Dey 1370/February 1991.

21. Naficy, 'Veiled Voice and Vision in Iranian Cinema: the Evolution of Rakhshan Banietemad's Films', in *Ladies and Gentlemen, Boys and Girls: Gender in Film at the End of the 20th Century*, edited by Murray Pomerance, New York: State University of New York Press, 2001, pp. 36–53.

22. Naficy, interview with Bahram Baizai, Houston, 5 November 1993.

23. Moruzzi, Norma Clair. 'Women's Space/Cinema Space: Representation of Public and Private in Iranian Films', paper presented at the Middle East Studies Association conference, Chicago, 3–6 December 1998, p. 7.

24. Naficy, 'Making Films with an Accent: Iranian Émigré Cinema,' in *Framework*, Autumn 2002, pp. 15–41.

25. Naficy, *An Accented Cinema: Exilic and Diasporic Filmmaking*, Princeton: Princeton University Press, 2001.

26. Naficy, 'Parallel Worlds', in *Shirin Neshat*. Vienna/London: Kunsthalle Wien/Serpentine Gallery, 2000, pp. 42–53.

27. 'Iranian Avant-Garde Cinema and the Films of Ghazel', in *Women in Iranian Cinema*, edited by Richard Tapper and Laura Mulvey, London: I.B. Tauris, forthcoming.

Selected Writings about the Veil

" Surah XXIV Light

31. And tell the believing women to lower their gaze and be modest, and to display of their adornment only that which is apparent, and to draw their veils over their bosoms, and not to reveal their adornment save to their own husbands or fathers or husbands' fathers, or their sons or their husbands' sons, or their brothers or their brothers' sons or sisters' sons, or their women, or their slaves or male attendants who lack vigour, or children who know naught of women's nakedness. And let them not stamp their feet so as to reveal what they hide of their adornment. And turn unto Allah together, O believers, in order that ye may succeed.

Surah XXXIII The Clans

53. O ye who believe! Enter not the dwellings of the Prophet for a meal without waiting for the proper time, unless permission be granted you. But if ye are invited, enter, and, when your meal is ended, then disperse. Linger not for conversation. Lo! That would cause annoyance to the Prophet, and he would be shy of (asking) you (to go); but Allah is not shy of the truth. And when ye ask of them (the wives of the Prophet) anything, ask it of them from behind a curtain. That is purer for your hearts and for their hearts....

59. O Prophet! Tell thy wives and thy daughters and the women of the believers to draw their cloaks close round them (when they go abroad). That will be better, that so they may be recognized and not annoyed. Allah is ever Forgiving, Merciful. "

Verses from the Quran. Extracts from Marmaduke Pickthall, *The Meaning of the Glorious Koran*, New York: Dorset Press, n.d.

" I came to realize during the course of my research on the subject that veiling is a rich and nuanced phenomenon, a language that communicates social and cultural messages, a practice that has been present in tangible form since ancient times, a symbol ideologically fundamental to the Christian, and particularly the Catholic, vision of womanhood and piety....

A Persian miniature of the sixteenth century depicts the first encounter between Prophet Muhammad and Khadija. He is on a camel, his face is white-veiled, and a nimbus of flames over his head marks his special sacred status.... She [Khadija] was the first believer in his [Muhammad's] visions and revelations and became the first follower of Islam.

As far as is presently known, Islam did not invent or introduce the custom of veiling. Veiling for men and women had existed in the region prior to Islam – in Hellenic, Judaic, Byzantine, and Balkan cultures. Whether by adoption, reinvention or independent invention, veiling in Arab social systems has evolved a distinct function and characteristic meaning from that in the northern Mediterranean regions. "

Fadwa El Guindi, *Veil: Modesty, Privacy and Resistance*, Oxford: Berg, 1999, preface, p. xii and p. 189.

Selected Writings about the Veil

Sassoferrato, *The Virgin in Prayer*, 1609–85. Oil on canvas, 73 x 57.7cm. © National Gallery.

Above: Rogier van der Weyden, *The Magdalen Reading* (detail), *c.* 1399–1464. Oil on mahogany, 61.6 x 54.6cm. © National Gallery.

Right: Miniature from *Ishaq an-Nisapurai*, Qisas al-Anbiya', Iran, *c.* 1560. Reproduced by kind permission of the Trustees of the Chester Beatty Library, Dublin.

" The veil has perhaps two advantages for women. In a country where little notice is taken of them in general, it is certainly a sort of subtle coquetry, although it is rarely used since they hardly ever go out. However, by showing nothing, everything is left to be guessed at, and a lively imagination will go far beyond reality. The veil, therefore, excites the desires.

A more real advantage of the veil is that it completely covers the face. With us a girl who is ugly can try for a long time, and perhaps forever, to find a husband. The veil saves women from such disappointments, but causes some for the husbands. Here you never know the face of the woman you are to marry, and the surprise of the husband when he sees for the first time the face of his wife after the wedding feast, if it is occasionally a pleasant one can often be very painful. It is true that he can seek consolation very quickly, either by taking another wife or by seeking an immediate divorce. But thanks to the veil, the woman has been married; at least she is sure that her ugliness will not force her to remain an old maid. "

J. Barthélemy Saint-Hilaire, *Lettres sur l'Egypte*, 1857, pp. 147–48.

" The women wear the universal loose, baggy gown of white or dark blue cotton, and over the face a white mask in which is a small openwork space for the eyes. The disguise is so complete, that one might pass his own wife or sister in the street without recognising her. It is said that this offers the greatest facility for intrigue, to which these Mahometan women are very much inclined. In the bazaars, especially those devoted to silks and wearing apparel, you see great numbers of females chaffering with the shopkeepers. But the men pass them by without notice, as it is impossible to tell, unless they choose to raise the corner of their veils, whether they are white or black, ugly or beautiful. "

William Perry Fogg, *Travels and Adventures in Egypt, Arabia, and Persia*, n.d., p. 172. (Travelling in 1874)

Zorah, Aïcha, Fathma,
late 19th–early 20th century.
Postcard. Collection Michket
Krifa.

Above: *Fillettes Bedouines*
(Bedouin Girls), late 19th–
early 20th century. Postcard.
Collection Michket Krifa.

Below: *Femmes Mauresques
en Promenade* (Moorish Women
Out Walking), late 19th–
early 20th century. Postcard.
Collection Michket Krifa.

" And how pretty they look, these women draped like phantoms in their black silks. Their long veils do not completely hide them, as do those of the Moslems. They are simply placed over their hair and leave uncovered the delicate features, the gold necklet and the half-bared arms that carry on their wrists thick twisted bracelets of virgin gold. Pure Egyptians as they are, they have preserved the same delicate profile, the same elongated eyes, as mark the old goddesses carved in bas-relief on the Pharaonic walls. But some, alas, amongst the young ones have discarded their traditional costume, and are arrayed *à la franque*, in gowns and hats. And such gowns, such hats, such flowers! The very peasants of our meanest villages would disdain them. Oh! Why cannot someone tell these poor little women, who have it in their power to be so adorable, that the beautiful folds of their black veils give to them an exquisite and characteristic distinction, while this poor tinsel, which recalls the mid-Lent carnivals, makes of them objects that excite our pity. "

Pierre Loti, *Egypt*, n.d., p. 111.

" Those old women squatting on the floor, with about five hairs, dyed a bright orange colour, are really disagreeable. They have harsh voices and they make an irritating noise. How thankful they ought to be for the veiling institution. "

Isobel Burton, *The Inner Life of Syria, Palestine, and the Holy Land*, 1875, vol. 1, pp. 145–46.

Femme Arabe. Femme Turque
(Turkish and Arab Woman in
Traditional Costume), 1860–80.
Albumen print. © V&A Picture
Library.

Gervais Courtellement et Cie,
*Moorish Women of Algiers,
Algiers*, before 1895. Henry
Balfour Collection, Pitt Rivers
Museum, University of Oxford.

" An observer might think that I now maintain the veil should be completely dispensed with – but this is not the case. I still defend the use of the veil and consider it one of the permanent cornerstones of morality. I would recommend, however, that we adhere to its use according to Islamic law, which differs from our present popular traditions. Our people are ostentatious in their caution and in their interpretations of what they believe to be the application of the law, to the extent that they presently exceed the limits of the Shari'a and have harmed the nation's interests.

My observations on this topic also indicate that Westerners have gone too far in the exposure of their women so that it is difficult for a Western woman to guard herself from sensuous desires and unacceptable shameful feelings. We, on the other hand, have gone to extremes in veiling our women and prohibiting them from appearing unveiled before men, to such an extent that we turn women into objects or goods we own. We have deprived them of the mental and cultural advantages that are their natural due as human beings. The legal veil, however, is somewhere between these two extremes.

I sense that a reader who has followed my reasoning thus far and who shares my viewpoint on the upbringing of women may resist with all his strength my proposition for returning to the veil's legal limitations. That person may resort to all the incorrect information he has internalised from the traditions of a society that reflects the ideas of many previous generations. He may therefore defend the status quo. Yet despite his effort to defend this tradition, and his pains to preserve it, it will not continue in its present form much longer....

Any person familiar with history knows that the veil played a role in the lives of women of other parts of the world. In his definition of the word 'veil', Larousse[1] wrote: 'Greek women used the veil when they went out; they hid their faces behind one of its ends as women in the Eastern nations do now.' And:

After Christianity was introduced to various countries, it perpetuated the use of the veil. Thus women covered their heads when they went out and during the time of prayer. Women also used the veil in the Middle Ages, especially during the ninth century. The veil at that time was wrapped around a woman's shoulders and almost dragged on the ground. This custom continued up to the thirteenth century, when women began to change its form, until it reached its present state – a thin fabric to protect the face from dust and cold. However, the veil continued to be used in Spain and in those American countries which were colonized by Spain.

This quotation demonstrates that the veil is not a custom peculiar to us. Muslims did not invent it. It was a prevalent custom in many nations, and its disappearance was the result of the societal changes which accompanied the change and progress of civilization. This important topic should also be considered from our religious and social perspectives.

The Religious Perspective
Had the Shari'a included specific passages to advocate the use of the veil as it is known now among Muslims, I would not have researched the topic. I would not have written a single letter contrary to those writings, however harmful they might have initially appeared, because heavenly orders should be obeyed without question, research, or discussion. However, the Shari'a does not stipulate the use of the veil in this manner. This custom is a produce of the interactions among nations. Muslims were attracted to the use of the veil, approved it, exaggerated its use, and dressed it up in religious raiment, just as other harmful customs have become firmly established in the name of religion, but of which religion is innocent. I therefore find no reason to avoid examining this topic; in fact, I believe that

it is our duty to become completely familiar with it, to identify the legal Islamic perspective, and to demonstrate the need for changing the present tradition....

Islamic law has given the same rights to women as to men. It makes them responsible for the civil and criminal consequences of their behaviour, and gives them the right to administer their finances and dispose of them. How then is it possible for a man to conclude business contracts with a woman without seeing her or having proof of her identity?

It is a very peculiar and difficult thing to prove the identity of a woman who is present but totally covered from head to foot or concealed behind a curtain or door. The man is told, for instance: here is the person who wishes to sell her house, or to appoint you as her proxy for marriage. The woman may state 'I have sold' or 'I have appointed', and the man is expected to be satisfied by the testimony of two witnesses, strangers or relatives, that she, as the identified person, has indeed sold or appointed. In these situations there is no dependable guarantee. Numerous legal cases demonstrate that cheating and forgery can easily take place in such circumstances. How often do we learn that a woman has been married without her knowledge, or that she has leased her property without being aware of it, or that she may even have been dispossessed of all that she owns and is ignorant of it? All this can occur because she is veiled and because men have taken charge of her affairs and come between her and those with whom she is dealing.

How can a poor woman who is veiled take on a business or trade and earn a livelihood? How can a veiled maid render adequate service in a house in which there are men? How can a business woman administer her affairs in the midst of men? How can a veiled peasant woman cultivate her land or reap her crop? How can a veiled worker who has hired herself out as a builder possibly build a house or anything else?

God created this world and gave human beings mastery over it so that they could enjoy the benefits according to what they can achieve. God granted human beings privileges for administering this world, but He also placed limitations on them. Thus God established equality between men and women regarding their obligations and privileges. God did not divide the universe, making one part of it to be enjoyed by women alone and another to be enjoyed by men, working in it segregated from women. In fact, He created the burdens of life to be shared and controlled by both men and women. How can a woman enjoy all the pleasures, feelings, and power that God created for her, and how can she work in the universe if she is banned from the sight of any man except a blood relative or some other man to whom she cannot be married according to Islamic law? Undoubtedly, this is not what the Shari'a meant, and it should not be allowed by either law or reason. Thus we see that necessity has changed the use of the veil among most classes of Muslims. This is apparent among maids, working women, villagers and even Bedouin women. All these women are Muslim – indeed they may be more religious than the city-dwellers.

If a woman's presence is required in a legal situation, why allow her to conceal her face? For years, both adversaries and judges paid no attention to this issue – they were lenient and allowed a woman to appear before them veiled. She could be a claimant, a defendant, or a witness, and the judges apparently surrendered to tradition. The danger with this leniency, which I think we cannot tolerate, is quite obvious: there is no positive method by which a veiled person can be identified. This situation lends itself easily to fraud. Every man who opposes a woman in litigation should be concerned about the proof of identity of his adversary, which is especially important in the context of the legal validity of her statement. I find it unacceptable for a judge to give a verdict about a

Gaëtan de Clérambault,
*Morocco. Province of
Casablanca. Azemmour.
Draped Costume*, 1918–34.
Photograph, 16 x 23cm.
Collection Musée de l'Homme,
Paris.

Gaëtan de Clérambault,
*Morocco. Province of Fes. Fes
Bali. Morphology of Draped
Costume*, 1918–34. Photograph,
28 x 39cm. Collection Musée
de l'Homme, Paris.

person whose face is veiled. I also consider it unacceptable for a judge to listen to a witness whose face is veiled. In fact, a judge's first responsibility is to verify the identity of the witness and the identity of the adversary, especially in criminal cases. Otherwise, why ask the name, age, occupation, and date of birth, as required by law? What use is it to know all these facts if the person's identity is not verified? The wisdom of the law is obvious when it asks that a woman uncover her face while she is a witness, for it allows the judge to scrutinize facial expressions, thus enabling him to better evaluate the testimony of the witness.

The disadvantages of veiling are without a doubt the reason the Shari'a allows the woman to uncover her face and her palms. I am not asking for more than what the Shari'a allows.

Religious leaders of various schools agree that it is possible for a man who is asking for the hand of a woman in marriage to see the woman he wishes to marry. An instance was quoted about the Prophet, God bless him and grant him salvation. In conversation with one of his followers who had asked for a woman's hand in marriage, he asked, 'Have you seen the woman?' The man answered, 'No.' The Prophet then responded, 'Go and see her. It is appropriate for you to become familiar with one another.'

These are the sayings of the Quran, the Prophetic tradition, and our religious leaders. They clearly demonstrate that God has allowed women to uncover their faces and palms for obvious reasons that can be understood by whoever wishes to understand them.

The judgment of the Shari'a is easy for both men and women to understand and reveals that men and women should not be separated by a veil, for it limits their interaction and hinders them in their work, whether it be authorized by the law or by life's necessities.

Furthermore, I do not believe that the veil is a necessary part of desirable behavior for women. There is no basis for such a claim. What is the relation between desirable behavior and exposing or veiling the face of a woman? What is the basis for discriminating against women? Is it not a produce of an individual's intentions and work rather than of external appearances and clothes?

The fear of temptation, addressed by almost every line written on the subject, is a matter close to the hearts of distrustful men. Women should not concern themselves with it nor ask to know anything about it. Whoever fears temptation, whether man or woman, should avert his or her glance. The instructions that appear in the precious verses about averting one's gaze apply to both men and women. This proves clearly that it is no more appropriate for a woman to cover her face than for a man to cover his.

How strange! If men feared that women would be tempted, why were not men ordered to wear the veil and conceal their faces from women? Is a man's will considered weaker than a woman's? Are men to be regarded as weaker than women in controlling their desires? Is a woman considered so much stronger than a man that men have been allowed to show their faces to the eyes of women, regardless of how handsome or attractive they are, while women are forbidden to show their faces to men from the fear that men's desires may escape the control of their minds, and they may thus be tempted by any woman they see, however ugly or disfigured she be? Any man who claims this viewpoint must then admit women always be placed under the protection of men? If however, this viewpoint is incorrect, what justifies this traditional control over women's lives?

The veil and the gauze face-cover actually increase the risk of temptation. The thin, white, gauze face-cover reveals the good features and hides the blemishes; the veil conceals the tip of the nose, the mouth and the jaws, and reveals the forehead, temples, eyebrows, eyes, cheeks and sides of the neck. These two coverings are in reality part of the ornaments worn by women that incite an onlooker's desires. They prompt him to wish to discover more of what is concealed after he has been tempted by the large area exposed. If a woman's face were uncovered, it is possible that her total appearance might turn glances away from her.

Temptation is not provoked by exposing some parts of a woman's body. In fact, the main causes of temptation are the revealing movements of a woman's body as she walks and the actions that reflect what is in her mind. The gauze face-cover and the veil, which hide a woman's identity, allow her to reveal what she wishes to reveal and to act in a manner that incites desire. She need not be concerned that anyone might identify her and report that so-and-so, or the wife of so-and-so, was doing such-and-such. She can accomplish whatever she desires under the protection of her veil. If her face were uncovered, her family status or her own honor would restrain her from initiating any provocative behaviour that might attract attention to herself.

In truth, the gauze face-cover and the veil are not part of the Shari'a, in terms either of piety or of morality. They have been handed down to us from ancient traditions that preceded Islam and have continued to survive. The proof is that this tradition is unknown in many other Islamic countries, and it is still a custom in many Eastern countries that do not claim Islam as their religion. Covering the bosom is part of Islamic law – there are clear admonitions about this – but nothing is mentioned about covering the face....

The Social Perspective

In my foregoing discussion I have suggested a change in the use of the veil and a return to its use as identified by the ordinances of the Shari'a, because we are attached to Islamic traditions and respect them. I am not in any way requesting this change because we wish to imitate for the sake of imitation Western nations and their traditions and conditions, nor simply because it is a new idea worth consideration. I believe that the Islamic legal tradition reflects the temperament and feelings that bind the members of our society. I do not regard our Islamic tradition like an item of clothing to be changed daily. My suggestion for a return to the legal use of the veil is based on my belief that this change would greatly improve our way of life. It is not my position to approve or denounce one thing or another simply on the basis of good or bad taste. My intent, however, is to support an acceptable context for women's lives, which implies an acceptable context for men's lives too....

The veil is one of the most important issues influencing the affairs of our country. If anyone allows himself to follow his emotions and conform to tradition, he will be able to consider the veil only through its favourable guise. Such a person has become accustomed to the use of the veil; it has become a familiar sight for him. Since his childhood he has been surrounded by it – he grew up and lived among veiled women. He inherited this tradition from his fathers and grandfathers and thus does not question its use. He does not consider the veil intellectually, but responds to it quite mechanically, and likes it instinctively. If, on the other hand, such a person removes himself from those factors that influenced the development of his feelings, if he discards those garments inherited from his predecessors, if he explores the topic objectively from all its facets and is influenced primarily by empirical data, then he will be able to perceive that it is impossible for a woman to exist fully unless she can control her own life. If such a person forms his opinion on the basis of personal observation, and if he is among those who search for truth, taking a stand on the basis of their findings, he will endorse the truth because for him truth occupies an important and significant position. If such a person does not fool himself through the adornment and embellishment of the hypothetical, but listens to the voice of a sound conscience, he will prefer it to all other views regardless of how prevalent those views are among those around him. At that point such a person will realize that a woman cannot be whole unless she enjoys the freedom granted her by the law and by her innate disposition. In addition, he will understand her potential and her need to develop it to the maximum. He will also realize that the veil as we know it is a great hindrance to a woman's progress, and indeed to a country's progress. **"**

Qasim Amin, 'Women and the Veil', *The Liberation of Women* and *The New Woman: Two Documents in the History of Egyptian Feminism*, translated by Samiha Sidhom Peterson. Cairo: The American University in Cairo Press, 2000, pp. 35–62. *The Liberation of Women* was first published in Arabic in 1899.

Note
1. Pierre Athanase Larousse, French grammarian, lexicographer, and encyclopedist, 1817–75

" Consider a veiled woman walking on the road accompanied by a servant. Right away you will see that the servant knows he has authority and is in charge. He walks ahead, and she follows. His silent language seems to say: 'I have been entrusted with this weak, ignorant being, and I am expected to watch her, guard her, and protect her.' Or watch them as they approach a group of coarse, ignorant men and notice the loud indecent expressions that they use with no consideration for these passers-by. Sometimes they bump up against her or touch her with their hands, although she has not made any suspicious movement that would cause them to accost her or arouse their repulsive actions. Why does a woman remain patient, silent, and fearful in the face of such an attack by men, and why does she not proceed to defend herself? Why is it that these men do not use their abominable language and atrocious actions with an unveiled woman? Is it because veiled women are more attractive to men than unveiled women? Certainly not. It is because men have fixed in their minds the idea that the veil and the silken wrap are badges of ignorance and weakness and signs of gullibility. They have seen in their own families that a woman is not respected, that she does not respect herself, that she is easily led and liable to weakness, that she will follow a man at the first sign or word he gives her, and that she fears men and does not dare to chastise them. So they scorn her, they have the nerve to humiliate her, and they are accustomed to respect a veiled woman only when she is accompanied by a man, even if that man is a eunuch!...

The veil, originally intended for wives only, was finally extended to daughters, sisters, and indeed all women, because every woman either is a wife, was a wife, or will become a wife. Veiling is the symbol of ancient ownership, and is one of the vestiges of the barbaric behavior that characterized human life for generations. It existed before it was realized that a person should not be owned simply because she was a female – just as people with black skin should not be slaves for the white man.

It is not unusual for the tradition of the veil to continue even after the cause that brought it about has disappeared – that is, after women have been removed from man's ownership. God's laws of creation dictate that the change from one state to another is gradual, and the change may not be noticed by those who undergo it. People often think it is impossible to change from the stage they are at, even thought they are already moving away from it and progressing towards a different one, either better or worse, without realizing it. Finally, when the transformation is complete, it becomes apparent that they have reached the stage they had earlier denied.

When men's right of ownership over women appeared, the customary law of gradual change required women to live in an intermediate stage between slavery and freedom, a condition where they were considered incomplete and imperfect human beings. It was too difficult for a man to consider a woman his equal, when the previous day she had been his property, so he preferred to place her in a position lower than the one he occupied. Men also claimed that when God created the human race, He gave intelligence and virtues to men but deprived women of these gifts. A woman's weakness, her lack of intelligence, and her proneness to carnal desires made it necessary for her to be dependent on men's power and to be separated from men, secluded in her house and veiled whenever she went out so that she would not seduce men with her beauty or deceive them with her feminine wiles. They also implied that she was not capable of moral or intellectual development, and must therefore remain in ignorance.

This is the secret behind the imposition of the veil upon women and for its continued existence. The first step for women's liberation is to tear off the veil and totally wipe out its influence....

Let us also assume for the sake of debate that veiling women safeguards them from corruption. Is such an argument sufficient to deprive women of their freedom? If it is men's actions toward women that are the cause of immorality, why is it that the woman's freedom is trampled while the man's freedom is respected? Is justice different for men and women? Are there two rights – a man's right and a woman's right? Is not everyone who is entrusted with the ability to choose entitled to choose and to act however he wishes as long as his actions do not exceed the Shari'a? **,,**

Qasim Amin, 'A Woman's Obligation to Herself', *The Liberation of Women* and *The New Woman: Two Documents in the History of Egyptian Feminism*, translated by Samiha Sidhom Peterson. Cairo: The American University in Cairo Press, 2000, pp. 132–37. *The New Woman* was first published in Arabic in 1900.

" Men criticise the way we dress in the street. They have a point because we have exceeded the bound of custom and propriety. We claim we are veiling, but we are neither properly covered nor unveiled. I do not advocate a return to the veils of our grandmothers because it can rightly be called being buried alive, not *hijab* nor correct covering. The woman used to spend her whole life within the walls of her house not going out into the street except when she was carried to her grave. I do not, on the other hand, advocate unveiling, like Europeans, and mixing with men, because they are harmful to us....

If we had been raised from childhood to go unveiled and if our men were ready for it I would approve of unveiling for those who want it. But the nation is not ready for it now. Some of our prudent women do not fear to mix with men, but we have to place limits on those who are less prudent because we are quick to imitate and seldom find our authenticity in the veil....

Veiling should not prevent us from breathing fresh air or going out to buy what we need if no one can buy it for us. It must not prevent us from gaining an education nor cause our health to deteriorate....

If I cannot find anyone but a man to teach me should I opt for ignorance or unveiling in front of that man along with my sisters who are being educated? Nothing would force me to unveil in the presence of the teacher. I can remain veiled and still benefit from the teacher.... If illness causes me to consult a doctor and there is no woman doctors should I abandon myself to sickness, which might be right but could become complicated, through neglect or should I seek help from a doctor who would cure me? "

Bahithat al-Badiya. Extracts from 'A Lecture in the Club of the Umma Party', 1909. Published in Margot Badran and Miriam Cooke (eds), *Opening the Gates: A Century of Arab Feminist Writing*, London: Virago, 1990.

" Five years ago we never walked a step; now we not only saunter through the bazaar, but go to a big dressmaker's in Pera.... But not only in the bazaar do we walk; we have walked in the magnificent newly laid-out park, where women are allowed for the first time to walk in a park where there are men. The men, I must say, have not yet grown accustomed to the new and extraordinary state of things, and vie with the Levantine 'mashers' in their desire to see the features under the veil. It is not a very comfortable experience for the Turkish woman, but it is the darkness before the dawn....

Is it [the veil] protection or is it not? Halide-Hanum considers that it creates between the sexes a barrier which is impossible when both sexes should be working for the common cause of humanity. It makes the woman at once the 'forbidden fruit', and surrounds her with an atmosphere of mystery which, although fascinating, is neither desirable nor healthy. The thicker the veil, the harder the male stares. The more the woman covers her face, the more he longs to see the features which, were he to see but once, would interest him no more.

Personally I find the veil no protection. In my hat I thread my way in and out of the cosmopolitan throng at Pera. No one speaks to me, no one notices me, and yet my mirror shows I am not more ugly than the majority of my sex. But when I have walked in the park [as] a veiled woman, what a different experience. Even the cold Englishman has summoned up courage and enough Turkish to play compliments to our 'silhouettes'. "

Grace Ellison. Extracts from *An Englishwoman in a Turkish Harem*, London: Methuen, 1915.

Nile Cruise to Luxor:
The Sidki Family, Egypt, 1914.
Photographer unknown,
collection Rachid Ismail/FAI.
© Fondation Arabe pour l'Image.

Scènes et Types. Femme Voilée
(Veiled Woman), early 20th
century. Postcard. Collection
Michket Krifa.

“ What are these unbecoming cloaks and veils?
They are shrouds for the dead, not for those alive
I say: 'Death to those who bury women alive'
If a few poets add their voices to mine
A murmur of discontent will start
With it women will unveil
They'll throw off their cloak of shame, be proud
Joy will return to lives
Otherwise, as long as women are in shrouds
Half the nation is not alive. ”

Mirzade-ye 'Eshqi (1894–1924)

Taken from 'Ali Akbar Moshir-Salimi (ed.), *Koliyat-e Mosavar-e Eshqi*.
Tehran: Sepehr, 1978, p. 218.

“ On the door of a traveller's inn
A woman's face was drawn in ink

From a reliable source of news
The turban-wearers heard the news

'Woe to our faith,' they said
'People saw a woman's face unveiled'

From inside the mosque in haste
To the front of the guesthouse they raced

Faith and order at the speed of light
Were disappearing when the believers arrived

One brought water, another dirt
With a veil of mud they covered the face

Honour, scarce gone with the wind
With a few fistfuls of mud was saved

Religious laws thus saved from danger
They returned to their homes to rest

With a careless mistake, the savage crowd
Like a roaring lion was jumping about

With her face unveiled, completely bare
Her chastity they tore apart

Her beautiful, alluring lips
Like a sugar candy they sucked and sucked

All of them, the men in town
To the sea of sin were drawn

The doors of paradise stood shut
The whole lot was hellward bound

The day of Judgement was at hand
Even the horn was blown at once

Birds from their nests, beasts from their lairs,
Even the stars in the sky went wild

Thus, before creator and created
The religious scholars remained exonerated

With saviours such as this bunch
Why are people still so cynical? ”

Iraj Mirza (1874–1925)

From Mohammad Ja'far Mahjub (ed.), *Iraj Mirza*.
Tehran: Andisheh, 1974, p. 177.

"I have seen many intellectuals of the nations where women are still veiled advocating unveiling, but I haven't seen anyone in the unveiled nations advocating or preferring the veil. That is, I haven't seen anyone who has tried unveiling and then has preferred the veil. Even if some westerner in his hypocritical words makes the veil appear in a favourable light, he is only pleased with the beauty of the oriental veil while at the same time he would reject the veiling of his mother, wife, sisters, and daughters because of the harm in the veil he favours for others....

It is inconceivable that we claim to be defenders of honour while the veil is our strongest shield. We must understand as everyone else does that honour is rooted in the heart and chastity comes from within and not from a piece of transparent material lowered over the face.

We have to realise, as the advanced unveiled world does, that good behaviour and honour come from sound upbringing grounded in noble principles and virtues. We are shortsighted if we think that the veil keeps evil away from women and that those in the rest of the world exceeding one and a half billion are all in the wrong while we are in the right....

The Prophet, God bless him, said, 'I was sent to help you attain the highest morality.' Does not the highest morality come from the soul? Pieces of cloth over faces shall never be a measure of morality....

Unfortunately, if the veil (*hijab*) implies the inability of the woman to protect herself without it, it also reveals that man, however well brought up and in spite of supporting the woman, is a traitor and a thief of honour; his evil should be feared and it is better that the woman escapes from him....

Does the woman who escapes from you, or approaches you lowering the veil over her face, or turns her back on you, confirm your high status, as she might think and say and you might think and say, or is it a great insult? Does this constitute the woman's decorum, chastity and modesty? If so, then men should not be without these precious attributes; let them wear veils and let them meet each other and meet women lowering veils over their faces the way women do."

Nazira Zain al-Din, extracts from *Unveiling and Veiling: Lectures and Views on the Liberation of the Woman and Social Renewal in the Arab World*, 1928. Translated by Ali Badran and Margot Badran and published in Margot Badran and Miriam Cooke (eds), *Opening the Gates: A Century of Arab Feminist Writing*, London: Virago, 1990.

Egyptian Women Speaking on Patriotism, Cairo, 24 May 1919.
© Bettmann/Corbis.

" After her experience at the Rome conference, she [Huda Sha'rawi] saw that the veil was the biggest obstacle in the way of progress of the Muslim Arab woman. Thus the veil had to fall so that with it the strongholds of reactionaries preventing women from being educated and participating in public life would fall.

Following this sound view, with her colleagues she decided to be the first to unveil. Upon their arrival by train at the station in the capital, they met those gathered there to receive them with their faces unveiled. When signs of disapproval became apparent in the crowd, women in the crowd immediately supported the unveiled women by also removing the veils from their faces and throwing them on the ground. Hence, the greatest victory in the history of the Arab woman....

This story that I tell you on the fiftieth anniversary of the Huda Shaarawi society is the gift that I present to the daughters of the new generation throughout the Arab world as a good example. Not only that, but to make clear that veiling is the greatest enemy of civilisation and advancement, and that nationalism cannot be worthy of mention nor respect if it does not exist in the form of courageous, constructive acts based on belief in values and morals. "

Amina Said. Extracts from *Feast of Unveiling. Feast of the Renaissance*, 1973. Translated by Ali Badran and Margot Badran and published in Margot Badran and Miriam Cooke (eds), *Opening the Gates: A Century of Arab Feminist Writing*, London: Virago, 1990.

" The first thing the foreign eye catches about Algerian women is that they are concealed from sight.

No doubt this very obstacle to sight is a powerful prod to the photographer operating in urban environments. It also determines the obstinacy of the camera operator to force that which disappoints him by its escape.

The Algerian woman does not conceal herself, does not play at concealing herself. But the eye cannot catch hold of her. The opaque veil that covers her intimates clearly and simply to the photographer a refusal. Turned back upon himself, upon his own impotence in the situation, the photographer undergoes *an initial experience of disappointment and rejection*. Draped in the veil that cloaks her to her ankles, the Algerian woman discourages the *scopic desire* (the voyeurism) of the photographer. She is the concrete negation of this desire and thus brings to the photographer confirmation of a triple rejection: the rejection of his desire, of the practice of his 'art,' and of his place in a milieu that is not his own.

Algerian society, particularly the world of women, is forever forbidden to him. It counterposes to him a smooth and homogenous surface free of any cracks through which he could slip his indiscreet lens.

The whiteness of the veil becomes the symbolic equivalent of blindness: a leukoma, a white speck on the eye of the photographer and on his viewfinder. *Whiteness is the absence of a photo, a veiled photograph, a whiteout, in technical terms.* From its background nothing emerges except some vague contours, anonymous in their repeated resemblance. Nothing distinguishes one veiled woman from another.

The veil of Algerian women is also seen by the photographer as a sort of perfect and generalized mask. It is not worn for special occasions. It belongs to the everyday, like a uniform. It instills uniformity, the modality of the impossibility of photography, its disappointment and deficiency of expression.

It will be noted that whenever a photographer aims his camera at a veiled woman, he cannot help but include in his visual field several instances of her. As if to photograph one of them from the outside required the inclusion of a *principle of duplication* in the framing. For it is always a group of veiled women that the photographer affixes upon his plate....

Here there is a sort of ironic paradox: the veiled subject – in this instance, the Algerian woman – becomes the purport of an unveiling.

But the veil has another function: to recall, in individualized fashion, the closure of private space. It signifies an injunction of no trespassing upon this space, and it extends it to another space, the one in which the photographer is to be found: public space.

These white islets that dot the landscape are indeed aggregates of prohibition, mobile extensions of an imaginary harem whose inviolability haunts the photographer-voyeur. They are scandalous, or at least perceived as being so. By their omnipresence, they revive frustration. They also recall the existence of the well-known pseudoreligious taboo of the Muslims: the figural depiction of the human body prohibited by Islam.

These veiled women are not only an embarrassing enigma to the photographer but an outright attack upon him. It must be believed that the feminine gaze that filters thought the veil is a gaze of a particular kind: concentrated by the tiny orifice for the eye, this womanly gaze is a little like the eye of a camera, like the photographic lens that takes aim at everything.

The photographer makes no mistake about it: he knows this gaze well; it resembles his own when it is extended by the dark chamber or the viewfinder. Thrust in the presence of a veiled woman, the photographer feels photographed; having himself become an object-to-be-seen, he loses initiative: *he is dispossessed of his own gaze.*

This varied experience of frustration is turned by the photographer into the sign of his own negation.

Algerian society, particularly the feminine world within it, threatens him in his being and *prevents him from accomplishing himself as gazing gaze.*

The photographer will respond to this quiet and almost natural challenge by means of a double violation: he will unveil the veiled and give figural representation to the forbidden. This is the summary of his only program or, rather, his symbolic revenge upon a society that continues to deny him any access and questions the legitimacy of his desire. The photographer's studio will become, then, a pacified microcosm where his desire, his scopic instinct, can find satisfaction. ❞

Malek Alloula, *The Colonial Harem*, translated by Myrna Godzich and Wlad Godzich. Manchester: Manchester University Press, 1987, pp. 7–14. First published in French as *Le Harem Colonial: Images d'un sous érotisme*, Geneva and Paris: Editions Slatkine, 1981.

Algiers. 22.12.26.

Mauresque d'Alger Voilée
(Veiled Moorish Woman from
Algiers), 1926. Postcard.
Collection Michket Krifa.

55. — Bédouine allaitant.   Photo Garrigues.

Bédouine Allaitant
(Bedouin Woman Breastfeeding),
1908. Postcard. Collection
Michket Krifa.

" I believe a woman should be full of excitement and intrigue like a film. In other words, she should conceal her nature and make men rely on their imagination in order to discover her.

Until a few years ago, Eastern women, because of the veil, were of and by themselves very alluring and this very allurement gave them incredible attraction. But gradually with their attempt to emulate Western women they unveiled themselves and decreased their sexual appeal. "

Ayatollah Morteza Mottahari quoting Alfred Hitchcock in *Mas'ale-ye Hejab* (The Issue of Veiling). Tehran: Enteshar, 1983, p. 56.

" No single item of clothing has had more influence on Western images of Middle Eastern women than the veil. This covering of the face was taken to symbolize Islam's special form of patriarchal subordination of women, despite the fact that veiling had been practised to various degrees in a number of other cultures: in pre-Islamic Arabia, as well as in ancient Assyria, Greece and Byzantium. Veiling was also practised in some Jewish and Christian communities living in countries where Islam was the dominant religion. Like seclusion, veiling – which could be described as a portable form of seclusion – was largely practised in peasant societies, and only among some Bedouin tribes.

The majority of Westerners, however, took little account of social nuances in the practice of veiling. They were simply fascinated or shocked by the sight of veiled women in city streets, visible yet invisible. For Western men in particular, the veil presented a challenge to the imagination. Writers, artists and photographers dwelt on the 'mysteries' which lay behind this piece of cloth....

Frustrated in the city streets, the photographer might turn to less concealed subjects, for instance, peasant and bedouin women who did not usually veil and who, when they were working or feeding their children, often had few inhibitions about exposing legs, arms and breasts. Westerners found this habit puzzling but eminently photogenic. Another way to break the taboo of the veil was to go back to the studio where the photographer, using models, had the power to decide what should be exposed and what covered....

Certainly most of the photographs of nude or semi-nude women taken in the Middle East in the nineteenth century stand within the first tradition [the nude as an erotic symbol, usually associated with sin, danger, corruption and death]. But the eroticism and danger which this genre aims to convey does not depend on the simple act of stripping off clothes, but rather on the juxtaposition of clothed and unclothed parts of the body, with the veil or headcovering often remaining as a motif. Above all, these photographs are assertions of sexual and cultural power, exposing, selectively and at will, parts of women's bodies, sometimes with an almost tangible sense of violence. The frequent suggestion of sexual danger in the semi-nude figure of the odalisque is, however, not accompanied by quite the same connotation of sin as can be found in comparable images of the seductress in the West. These photographs, like, many Orientalist paintings, are a transgression not of Western morality but of the rules and taboos of another culture, viewed as inferior to that of Europe....

In Algeria, where the Orientalist image of the veiled seductress had been developed from the beginning of the French occupation for the benefit of soldiers, colonists and tourists, the struggle over the social and political implications of the veil was sharpest. From the 1930s until the 1950s, the French made concerted efforts to engineer a variety of social changes in Algerian society, including the abolition of the veil. These efforts reinforced the growing nationalist movement in its belief that this was an attempt to sabotage and destroy the remaining cohesion of Algerian society, already undermined by colonial economic and settlement policies. The veil in this period therefore became a symbol of the continuity of national culture, a view forcefully expressed by Frantz Fanon, who combines the metaphors of cultural and sexual violence in his condemnation of French colonial policy. 🙸

Sarah Graham-Brown, *Images of Women, Portrayal of Women in Photography of the Middle East 1860–1950.* London: Quartet, 1987.

🙶 The concept of the word *hijab* is three-dimensional, and the three dimensions often blend into one another. The first dimension is a visual one: to hide something from sight. The root of the verb *hajaba* means 'to hide'. The second dimension is spatial: to separate, to mark a border, to establish a threshold. And finally, the third dimension is ethical: it belongs to the realm of the forbidden. So we have not just tangible categories that exist in the reality of the senses – the visual, the spatial – but also an abstract reality in the realm of ideas. A space hidden by a *hijab* is a forbidden space. 🙸

Fatima Mernissi, *Women and Islam: An Historical and Theological Enquiry,* trans. Mary Jo Lakeland, Oxford: Basil Blackwell, 1991.

❝ Writing, with its potential for public communication, for entering into the world of others, could be considered no less a transgression than unveiling. In both, a woman expresses/exposes herself publicly. Through both, an absence becomes a presence. Both are means of expression and communication: one gives her voice a body, the other gives her body a voice. Writing, like unveiling, makes a woman publicly visible and mobile....

Iranian male authors, too, have repeatedly complained of the agonies of veiling and have openly expressed the desire to unveil. The celebrated fourteenth-century poet, Hafez, said: 'Happy the moment when from my face I cast off the veil.' The great mystical poet, Jalal ed-Din Rumi (d. 1273), said: 'This is love: to fly heavenward / To rend, every instant, a hundred veils.' Their wish, interpreted by many as a mystical metaphor, can also be viewed as a more universal problem in literary creation. Is publishing an act of unveiling, or, on the contrary, an act of veiling to hide behind? Do we reveal or conceal the truth of ourselves in the poems we craft, in the stories we spin? Perhaps writers unveil only by spinning veils of another form. Perhaps the veil moves from the physical to other dimensions. Perhaps words are not only means of expression but also invisible walls we erect to contain the otherwise uncontainable.

Still, shouldn't we ask ourselves why the greatest of Iran's poets, like Hafez and Rumi, represent their own literary anxiety, their struggles with love and words, in terms of the woman's unveiling? Is the search for truth and love an act of dis-covering, dis-closing, un-veiling? Perhaps the anxieties attached to the confrontation of love and reality are displaced onto a woman's body and its nakedness. Perhaps the veil, because of its symbolic potency, becomes a vessel in which to place both the anxieties and the exhilarations of love and creativity. **❞**

Farzaneh Milani, *Veils and Words: The Emerging Voices of Iranian Women Writers*. London and New York: I.B. Tauris, 1992, pp. 6–7.

❝ My choice of the veil is one of the most important personal decisions of my life. I was at school thinking about applying to university.... In that kind of world I felt that it was important to dress so that people would know I was a Muslim.... My decision to wear the veil also ties into my feeling of coming from this different kind of background. We are a British family but because of Islam and our links with Pakistan we have different values and traditions from the families of my non-Muslim friends.... I would feel completely exposed without my veil. It is liberating to have the freedom of movement and to be able to communicate with people without being on show. It's what you say that's important not what you look like.... At the same time wearing the veil makes me feel special, it's a kind of badge of identity and a sign that my religion is important to me.... I find it easier to mix and get around in public and not be bothered by lecherous stares or worse. But these are just advantages of a certain style of dress which doesn't draw attention to the body or fit the Western stereotypes of sexy clothes. They don't have anything specific to do with Islam, they have more to do with being female in a sexist and male dominated society where women are judged by how they look.

Nadia, a British-Asian medical student who adopted the veil at the age of sixteen.

I did not think to wear the veil as a younger woman at home in Algiers, it was not important then. At that time my mother, aunts and sisters wore a western style of clothes and did not cover their hair or face.... When my husband and I came to France,... I had to find employment... and there was no question that I would not wear a veil.... It is important to me to keep my appearance private and not to be stared at by strange men and foreigners.... [Veiling] allows me more freedom and shows that I am a woman concerned about her modesty. The experience of being in a foreign place is unpleasant and difficult, and wearing the veil eases some of the problems.... Sometimes wearing the veil means that you attract the attention of the French people who hate Islam, but experiences like this make me more proud of being an Arab and a Muslim... you also feel safe when wearing the veil in any kind of situation – it is a protection as well as a sign of love of Islam.

Maryam, a middle-aged textile factory worker living in France.

Why have young girls started to cover themselves in this new type of veil and dress like old women? I think that it is just a trend, a fashion like any other.... Fifty years ago, girls were most interested in the fabrics, colours and designs which would attract a possible husband's interest... we only thought about clothes in this sense. It wasn't that *hijab* and modesty were unimportant, it was just that girls were not so serious about it.... I do not think that this new veiling is a religious duty. A woman's modest conduct is more important than what she wears.... Although I have this opinion about the new veil being a trend which is not an essential part of Islam, I am not against what it stands for if it means that society is becoming more concerned with morality and turning against some of the modern ways and Western values which started to take hold.... It is important for the Arab people to rediscover their own traditions and take pride in themselves.... We have become used to seeing Western women almost naked in our streets and if, because of this, our women want to cover themselves in the new veil, then it is a welcome protest against indecency and our overwhelming past interest in all things foreign. The women who adopt the new veil do so for a number of reasons, but it should not be a matter of law, but one of personal choice.

Fatima, a vegetable seller in Cairo, in her late seventies.

Extracts from Helen Watson, 'Women and the Veil: Personal Responses to Global Process', in Akbar S. Ahmed and Hastings Donnan (eds), *Islam, Globalization and Postmodernity*, London and New York: Routledge, 1994.

" On 18 September 1989, Leila Achaboun, Fatima Achaboun and Samira Saïdani – three schoolgirls of North African descent – were suspended from the Collège Gabriel-Havez, in the northern Parisian suburb of Creil, for refusing to remove the headscarves that they understood to be prescribed by Islamic tradition. The school's principal, Ernest Chenière, claimed to be acting in accordance with the Ferry laws of the 1880s, which first mandated the secular school system in France, and with legislation from the beginning of the century which prohibited the wearing of religious or political symbols and forbade proselytising there....

The incident was brought to the attention of Lionel Jospin, then Minister of Education, who overturned Chenière's decision on 25 October, insisting that although the French school system should discourage the wearing of the *hidjeb*, it had no right to exclude the girls on that basis....

The grand controversy, as trumpeted in the press, amounted to a face-off between the values of *égalité* and *laïcité*, two values long associated with the French republican tradition, and the tolerance of diversity, or what had come to be known in France in the 1980s as 'le droit à la différence'. Significantly, while those in the former camp directly attacked the premises of the 'right to difference', those in the latter camp failed to deconstruct their opponents' terms. As a result, the public defenders of diversity could not but advance their case on terms set by their opponents. That is, they were constrained to pleading for difference in spite of *égalité* and *laïcité*. In the story that unravelled in the French press, therefore, the big 'tohu-bohu' came down to a challenge posed by a piece of fabric – and all that could be associated with it – to the ostensibly time-honoured republican principles of secularism and individual rights. "

Diana R. Blank. Extracts from 'A Veil of Controversy: The Construction of a "*Tchador Affair*" in the French Press', in *Interventions: International Journal of Postcolonial Studies*, vol. 1, no. 4, London, Routledge, 1999.

Faisal Abdu'Allah

Faisal Abdu'Allah (born London, 1969) graduated with an MA in Fine Art from the Royal College of Art in London, where he continues to live and work. He practices in the media of photography, screen print and installations. Appropriating iconography from the media, religion and popular culture, Abdu'Allah deconstructs and challenges the stereotypical images of black people that have come to dominate collective and individual consciousness. Recent solo exhibitions include Chisenhale Gallery (London, 2003); The Agency (London, 2002); Horniman Museum (London, 2001); *Heads of State* (Margaret Harvey Gallery, Hertfordshire; Standpoint Gallery, London; and Middlesborough Art Gallery, 1997–98); and *Revelations* (Bonington Gallery, Nottingham, and 198 Gallery, London, 1995). Group exhibitions include B.I.G. Torino Biennale (Italy, 2002); ARCO Artfair (Spain, 2001); *Ecce Homo* (Kunsthal Rotterdam, The Netherlands, 2000); and *Transforming the Crown* (Studio Museum Harlem, New York, 1997–98).

Kourush Adim

Kourush Adim (born Iran, 1971) is an artist whose work plays on the poetry of the veil as part of the natural, physical landscape. A series of black and white photographic prints have at their centre a ghostly, veiled presence that haunts the empty rural landscape. He has participated in over fifty-five exhibitions and festivals, both in Iran and abroad, among them the 5th Poland Triennial (Majdanka, Poland, 1997); 2nd International Biennial of Photography (Tehran Contemporary Art Museum, Iran, 1996); 140th Edinburgh International Exhibition of Photography (Scotland, 2002); and *Regards Persans* (Espace Electra, Paris, 2001). He has contributed to a number of books, including illustrations for Christian Bobin, *La Présence Pure* (Cognac: Le Temps qu'il Fait, 1999); *The Shadow of Beautiful Hair on a Stone: A Book of Verse* (Ghoo Publications, 2002); and *The Ambiguous Presence of Meaning* (Mahriz Publications, 2001).

AES art group

AES art group was established in 1987 and comprises three Russian Jewish artists: Tatiana Arzamasova (born 1955), Lev Evzovich (born 1958) and Evgeny Svyatsky (born 1957), all of whom live and work in Moscow. Both Arzamasova and Evzovich graduated from the Moscow Architectural Institute and are interested in conceptual architecture, while Svyatsky graduated from the Moscow Polygraphic Institute, his practice focusing on book and advertising design, posters and graphic art. AES create imagined cityscapes of the leading Western metropolises – from New York to Paris, Rome to Sydney, Moscow to Berlin – in the year 2006, envisaging how they might appear under a different regime. Using wit and satire, AES's digitally manipulated images are storyboards reflecting the deep-rooted insecurities of today's postmodern, postcolonial, post-Cold War society. Selected solo exhibitions include *Le Roi des Aulnesa* (Galerie Knoll, Vienna, 2002); *AES. Islamic Project* (Galerie Sollertis, Toulouse, France, 2001); *AES Travel Agency to the Future – Islamic Project* (SIETAR Europe Congress 2000, Brussels, 2000); and *AES Nomade Makes Stop in New York* (Art in General, New York, 1999).

Jananne Al-Ani

An Iraqi-born artist living and working in London, Jananne Al-Ani investigates the representation of Middle Eastern women by late nineteenth-century and early twentieth-century European painters, photographers, travellers and writers. She is particularly interested in photographic studio portraits and the construction of fantastic tableaux which explore the Western fascination with the veil. Al-Ani studied Fine Art at the Byam Shaw School of Art and graduated with an MA in Photography from London's Royal College of Art in 1997. She has exhibited widely in Britain and abroad and has had solo shows at the Smithsonian Institution in Washington D.C. and the Imperial War Museum in London. Recent exhibitions include *Sans Commune Mesure: Image et Texte dans L'Art Actuel* (Musée D'Art Moderne Lille Métropole, France, 2002); *The Body as Territory*, curated by Michket Krifa for *Les Rencontres de la Photographie d'Arles* (France, 2002); and *Fair Play* (Danielle Arnaud Contemporary Art, London, 2001), which she co-curated with the artist Frances Kearney. Recent commissions include Film and Video Umbrella's *Identinet* web project (2002) in collaboration with the Arts Council of England and Channel 4 Television.

Ghada Amer

Ghada Amer is an Egyptian-born (1963) artist who lives in New York. Amer graduated from Institut des Hautes Etudes en Art Plastique in France (1991), having previously studied at Beaux-Arts, Nice, and the School of the Museum of Fine Arts, Boston. At first glance, Amer's works appear to be finely drawn, abstract and spontaneous automatist scribblings; on closer inspection, however, one discovers that they are, in fact, fragmented lines of figurative embroidery. Depicting the naked or scantily clad female body in the archetypal poses of pornography, the works evoke the ongoing contemporary discourse on the relationship between sexuality and gender. She has had recent solo exhibitions at Gagosian Gallery, (London, 2002); San Francisco Art Institute (2002); De Appel Foundation (Amsterdam, 2002); *Reading Between the Threads* (Henie Onstad Kunstsenter, Oslo; Kunst Palast, Düsseldorf, and Bildmuseet, Umeå, Sweden, 2001); *Encyclopedia of Pleasure* (Deitch Projects, New York, 2001); *Ghada Amer: Pleasure* (Contemporary Arts Museum, Houston, 2001); Rhona Hoffman Gallery (Chicago, 2001); CCC Tours (France, 2000); and *Intimate Confessions* (Tel Aviv Museum of Art, Israel, 2000).

Farah Bajull

Born in Iran, Farah Bajull graduated with an MA in Sculpture from the Royal College of Art in London, where she now lives and works. Drawing on the tradition of Western art practice that foregrounds performance and object-based work, Bajull's practice introduces specific cultural references. Her works represent a compelling merger of divergent visual forms, ranging from carefully constructed objects to stand-alone photographs, to imagery generated from her own performance documentation and video footage. Solo exhibitions include the *Digital Responses* series (V&A, London, 2002); *Untying the Knot* (TheSpace@inIVA, London, 2001); *Foreign Bodies* (Stephen Lawrence Gallery at the University of Greenwich, 2001); and *us and Them* (University of Hertfordshire, 2001). Group shows include *Melodrama* (Centro José Guerrero, Granada, Spain, 2002); and Artium Centro Museo Vasco de Arte Contemporaneo (Vitoria, Spain, 2002). Bajull has work in the Norton Foundation Collection and other private collections worldwide.

Samta Benyahia

Algerian French artist Samta Benyahia lives and works in Paris. Benyahia uses Arab Andalusian geometrical motifs and rosaces – called *fatima* (also the name of Muhammad's daughter) in Arabic – to explore issues of contrast, such as light/shade, female/male and inside/outside. She has been given a number of solo shows internationally, among them, the Institut Français (Alexandria, Egypt, 2003); Spacex Gallery (Exeter, UK, 2001–2); La Corte Arte Contemporanea (Florence, Italy, 2000); and Art in General (New York, 1996). Groups shows include *ARC* (Musée d'Art Moderne de la Ville de Paris, 2001) and the Havana Biennale (Cuba, 1994). Her work is held in, among other collections, the Bibliothèque Nationale in Paris, in the Musée National des Beaux-Arts in Algiers and in the Institut Français in Casablanca (Morocco).

Gaëtan de Clérambault

Gaëtan de Clérambault was born in France in 1872 and died in 1934. A psychiatrist, Clérambault was fascinated by the relationship between women and fabric. As a photographer, he went on to extend his research by taking images of veiled women (and occasionally men) in Morocco. He became increasingly obsessed by the drapes and forms created by the veil and the 'invisible gaze' of the veiled women he photographed, producing a huge body of photographs, many of which are now in the collection of the

Artists' Biographies

Musée de l'Homme, Paris. His photographs have been published in *Gaëtan Gatian de Clérambault: psychiatre et photographe* (Collection Les Empêcheurs de Penser en Rond, 1990).

Marc Garanger

Marc Garanger was a photographer before doing military service. The army insisted on taking identity photographs of all Algerians during the War of Independence (1954–62). Adopting a critical stance, Garanger took this chance to make artistic portraits in which he tried to reflect the beauty of Algerian women who were being faced with outrageous racism by the French government and army. Photographs of indigenous Americans by the famous American photographer Edward Curtis inspired the nature of the photographs Garanger took of these women. They are deeply disturbing images full of imminent violence, with the 'de-veiling' that the women experienced at the hands of the military being akin to rape. His photographs have been published in *Marc Garanger: Femmes Algériennes 1960* (Contrejour, 1982 and 1989; Atlantica, 2002).

Shadafarin Ghadirian

Shadi Ghadirian (born 1974) is a photographer who studied at Azad University and continues to live and work in Tehran, Iran. In addition to teaching photography, she works for the Museum of Photography; for an advertising company Simia nama; and for *Mahtab Magazine* for teenage girls. Inspired by photographs of the Qajar dynasty, Ghadirian has recreated a Qajar studio in her Tehran home. Having scrupulously choreographed the formal poses, she then adds televisions, vacuum cleaners and

bicycles. Consequently, the subtle gestures of the sitters carry complex and powerful social significance. She has exhibited recently at The Museum of Contemporary Art (Tehran, 2002); A Space Gallery (Toronto, 2001); FNAC (Paris, 2001); *Iranian Contemporary Art* (Barbican Art, London, 2001); London Guildhall University (2000); The Iranian Women's Studies Foundation (Worth Ryder Gallery, University of California, 2000); and Haus der Kulturen der Welt (Berlin, 2000).

Ghazel

Ghazel (born 1966, Tehran, Iran) now lives and works in Paris, France. She graduated in Visual Arts from the Ecole des Beaux-Arts de Nîmes in 1992 and in Film Studies from the Université Paul Valéry, Montpellier, in 1994. In her ongoing *Me* series, Ghazel re-enacts moments from her personal diary with the veil as her ever-present 'costume'. Each scene is accompanied by a caption in French or English, neither of which are her mother tongues. Full of irony and surreal humour, her performances highlight her position as an outsider both in the West and in Iran. Recent solo shows include *Wanted* (Salon Meschec Gaba, Palais de Tokyo, Paris, 2002); *Me 1997–2000* (Miroslav-Kraljevic Gallery, Zagreb, 2001); and *Sans Titre* (TRAC in FRAC, Montpellier, 1999). She has also exhibited at *Iranian Contemporary Art* (Barbican Art, London, 2001); *Regards Persans* (Espace Electra, Paris, 2001); and *Chronicle of Void and Beyond* (Golestan Gallery, Tehran, 1999), a joint project with Kaveh Golestan. She has work in the Musée National d'Art Moderne (Centre Georges Pompidou, Paris) and *Ghazel Me 1997–2000* was published to accompany her recent show in Zagreb (Milan Vranesic Publishers, 2001).

Emily Jacir

Born in Riyadh, Saudi Arabia (1970), of Palestinian parents, Emily Jacir lives and works in New York. Jacir studied under the Whitney Independent Study Programme, New York (1998–99), having first graduated from Memphis College of Art and the University of Dallas. Her mixed-media work addresses the unconscious markers of borders between territories, places, countries and states. *From Paris to Riyadh* is inspired by Jacir's memories of travelling to Saudi Arabia and watching her mother blacking out, with a marker pen, the exposed flesh of the models in fashion magazines. Recent exhibitions include *Unjustified* (Apex Art, New York, 2002); *Submerged* (Kunstbunker, Nuremberg, Germany, and Kuntshalle Exnergasse, Vienna, 2002); *Scattered Belongings* (Jordan National Gallery, Amman, Jordan, 2002); Sala di Consultazione, Biagiotti Arte Contemporanea (Florence, Italy, 2001); *Strangers/Etrangers* (PS1 Clocktower, New York, 2001); *Uncommon Threads* (Herbert Johnson Museum, Cornell University, New York, 2001); and *Made in Transit* (Vacancy Gallery, New York, 2001).

Ramesh Kalkur

Ramesh Kalkur (born 1969, Bangalore, India) studied Painting at the Faculty of Fine Arts, M.S. University, Baroda, and graduated on an Inlaks Foundation Scholarship with an MA in Painting from the Royal College of Art, London, in 1996. He made a series of photographs in which the main protagonist mimics the practical functions of the veil; the resulting hand movements suggest both gesticulated outward communication and defensive inward shielding. He has recently

exhibited at *11x11 Show of Paintings and Photographs* (Gallery Sumukha, Bangalore, 2002) and, in 1998, he had solo shows at Sakshi Art Gallery, Bangalore; British Council Gallery, Chennai; and Chitram Art Gallery, Cochin. His group exhibitions include *Five Steps* (Mermaid Theatre Gallery, London, 1996); *Territory* (Bangalore, 1998); 'Sthalapuranagalu (Bangalore, 1999); and *Flashback Flashforward* (Jehangir Art Gallery, Bombay, 1999).

Majida Khattari

A Moroccan-born artist who lives in Paris, Majida Khattari graduated from the Ecole des Beaux-Arts in Paris in 1995. Khattari stages fashion shows as highly political performance works which link Western high fashion to Islamic codes of dress and behaviour. Not simply designed to flatter the wearer, the garments she creates restrict movement and conspicuously conceal or reveal different parts of the body. Recently, her work has been shown at a catwalk performance at Centre Georges Pompidou (Paris, 2001); *Mixed Memory* (Kunstmuseum, Lucerne, Switzerland, 2000); *Heaven: New French Art* (Kunsthalle, Dusseldorf; Tate Gallery, Liverpool; and Setagaya Art Museum, Tokyo, 1999); and *Premises* (Guggenheim Museum Soho, New York, 1998–99).

Shirin Neshat

Shirin Neshat is an Iranian-born visual artist and film-maker living in New York City. An internationally acclaimed artist, her video installations deal with the tension of gender relations in the context of modern-day Iran as an Islamic state. Neshat is the winner of numerous awards, including the Infinity Award of ICP in New York (2002), the

Grand Prix of the Kwangju Biennial in Korea (2000) and the Golden Lion Award at the 48th Venice Biennale (1999). Among her most recent solo exhibitions are: Castello di Rivoli (Turin, Italy, 2002); The Walker Art Center (Minneapolis, 2002); Museum of Contemporary Art (Montreal, Canada, 2001); Kunsthalle (Vienna, 2000); Serpentine Gallery (London, 2000); The Art Institute of Chicago (1999); and Tate Gallery (London, 1998). She has been included in numerous international exhibitions and film festivals, including Documenta 11 (Germany, 2002); Sao Paulo Biennial (Brazil, 2002); The Whitney Biennial (2000); and the 48th Venice Biennale (Italy, 1999). Neshat has also received critical acclaim in publications such as *The New York Times*, *Le Monde*, *The Los Angeles Times*, *Art In America*, *Art Forum*, and *Art News*.

Harold Offeh

Harold Offeh (born 1977, Accra, Ghana) moved to England in 1980. Having first studied Critical Fine Art Practice at the University of Brighton, he graduated with an MA in Photography from the Royal College of Art, London, in 2001. Offeh is an artist who adopts humour and narrative in his work in order to unravel the complex relationships between ideas of race and representation. Using comic everyday and domestic scenes of frustration and alienation, Offeh presents a reality that is veiled or distorted through the use of a variety of photographic techniques. He was selected to exhibit in *New Contemporaries 2001* (Camden Arts Centre, London, and Northern Gallery for Contemporary Art, Sunderland) and the *10th East International* (Norwich Gallery, UK, 2000). He has also exhibited in a number of international shows including *Juncture* (Granary, Cape Town, South Africa, 2001); *Behind the Face* (Galleria Plastica, Bologna, Italy, 2001); and *Life. A Users Manual* (Baltic Sea Arts Centre, Gdansk, Poland, 2001). Solo exhibitions include *Harold Offeh* (Gasworks Gallery, London, 2002) and *Unfulfilled Desires* (Tablet Gallery, London, 2002). In 2003, he will be exhibiting at Tate Modern, London, as part of *In Focus: From Tarzan to Rambo*.

Gillo Pontecorvo
Born in 1919 in Pisa, Italy, Gillo Pontecorvo first attained international prominence for directing *Kapò* (1959), which earned him the 1960 Academy Award nomination for best foreign film. He went on to win the Golden Lion at the Venice Film Festival (and was nominated for an Academy Award as best director) for his film *The Battle of Algiers* (1965). The film plays with notions of objectivity by constructing a pseudo-documentary that captures the authenticity of newsreel footage with a scripted dramatic reconstruction using actors and members of the Algerian population. In *The Battle of Algiers*, the veil is seen as a symbol of resistance to French colonial oppression.

Zineb Sedira
Zineb Sedira is a French Algerian artist who graduated from the Slade School of Art and the Royal College of Art in London, where she now lives and works. The 'veiling of the mind' – a metaphor for the complex cultural positioning faced by her generation of Algerian women living in the West – is the basis for much of Sedira's dialogue. The issue of representation in Islam – non-figurative imagery – is also explored in her work and relates

to the idea of veiling and iconoclasm. She has exhibited extensively internationally, including at the 49th Venice Biennale and at biennales in Valencia, Spain, and Limerick, Ireland. In 2001, she won the Prix AFAA at *Rencontres de la Photographie Africaine de Bamako*. Recent solo shows include *Les Rencontres de la Photographie d'Arles* in France (2002) and The Agency (London, 2002); in 2003–4, Cornerhouse (Manchester, UK) will be launching a major touring solo show. Her work can be found in the collections of the Musée Réattu, Arles; the Fonds National d'Art Contemporain, Paris; the Centre Georges Pompidou, Paris; the Arts Council of England, London; the Victoria and Albert Museum, London; and the Gallery of Modern Art, Glasgow. Her work has been featured in numerous magazines and books, most recently *Blink* (Phaidon Press, 2002).

Elin Strand
Elin Strand (born 1970) is based in Stockholm, Sweden, but graduated from Goldsmiths College, London, in 2000. Originally from an architectural background, Strand works mainly with video, performance and installations to address notions of concealment, veiling and the act of drapery. She poses questions about masks and sexual identity, and about how sexual restrictions and conventions are censuring our individuality. Strand had a recent solo exhibition at Gallery Konstakuten (Stockholm, 2002) and has also shown her work at *Much Depends on the Viewer* (Vienna International Apartment, 2002); Rum46 (Århus, 2001); Goldsmiths College (London, 2000); Pump House Gallery (London, 2000); Peblinc Gallery (Copenhagen, 2000); and Chisenhale Gallery (London,

1999). In 2003, her work will be shown in *I Can See You But You Can't See Me* (Gothenburg Art Museum, Sweden), which she is also curating. The exhibition is based on her visits to Iran and on a cultural exchange project between Iran and Sweden. Strand is a member of the Art and Architecture group Great Eastern Hotel.

Mitra Tabrizian
Iranian-born photographer and film-maker Mitra Tabrizian is now based in London. Having graduated in Film and Photographic Arts at the University of Westminster, London, Tabrizian uses techniques associated with documentaries, reportage and advertising to analyse critically the ideological underpinnings that structure cultural identity, with a particular perspective on the politics of gender, class and race. Her collaboration with Andy Golding on the photographic series *The Blues* (1986–87) and the *Surveillance* series (1990) brought her to prominence as a cultural practitioner. Recent selected exhibitions and screenings include *The Third Woman* (Diaspora Film Festival, Toronto, 2002); *Inhabiting* (Gallery Lelong, New York, 2001); *London: Post Colonial City* (Architectural Association, London, 1999); and her solo show *Minimal Utopia* (Camera Austria, Graz, 1997). Tabrizian's writings and photo essays have been widely published in international journals and in a monograph *Correct Distance* (Cornerhouse Publications, 1990). Tabrizian currently teaches at the University of Westminster, London.

David A. Bailey is an artist, writer, curator and co-director of AAVAA (African and Asian Visual Artists Archive), London. He has curated a number of landmark exhibitions including *Mirage: Enigmas of Race, Difference and Desire* (ICA, London, 1995) and *Rhapsodies in Black: Art of the Harlem Renaissance* (Hayward Gallery, London; Arnolfini, Bristol; Mead Gallery, University of Warwick; M.H. de Young Memorial Museum, San Francisco; The Corcoran Gallery of Art, Washington D.C.; Los Angeles County Museum, Los Angeles; and Houston Museum of Fine Art, Houston, 1997–99).

Alison Donnell is Senior Lecturer in Postcolonial Literatures at Nottingham Trent University. She is joint editor of *Interventions: International Journal of Postcolonial Studies* and edited a special issue of the journal on 'The Veil: Postcolonialism and the Politics of Dress', *Interventions 1.4* (Routledge, 1999). She has recently edited the *Companion to Contemporary Black British Culture* (Routledge, 2002). As well as co-editing *The Routledge Reader in Caribbean Literature* (1996), she has written many articles and book chapters on Caribbean literature, particularly women's writing. Her book, *Critical Moments: Rereading Twentieth Century Caribbean Literature*, will be published by Routledge in 2004.

Reina Lewis is Senior Lecturer in Cultural Studies at the University of East London. She is author of *Gendering Orientalism: Race, Representation and Femininity* (Routledge, 1996) and co-editor, with Sarah Mills, of *Feminism and Postcolonial Theory* (Edinburgh University Press, 2002). She is currently completing *Feminisms in the Harem: Ottoman Women Write about the Harem* (I.B. Tauris, 2003) and *Middle Eastern and Western Feminisms: A Critical Sourcebook*, edited with Nancy Micklewright (I.B. Tauris, 2003).

Hamid Naficy is Nina J. Cullinan Professor of Art and Art History/ Film and Media Studies and Chair of Department of Art and Art History, Rice University, Houston. He has published extensively about theories of exile and displacement; exilic and diasporic cultures, films, and media; and Iranian, Middle Eastern and Third World cinemas. His recent English-language books include *An Accented Cinema: Exilic and Diasporic Filmmaking* (Princeton University Press, 2001); *Home, Exile, Homeland: Film, Media, and the Politics of Place* (editor, Routledge, 1999); *The Making of Exile Cultures: Iranian Television in Los Angeles* (University of Minnesota Press, 1993); and *Otherness and the Media: The Ethnography of the Imagined and the Imaged* (co-editor, Harwood Academic, 1993). His forthcoming *Cinema and National Identity: A Social History of the Iranian Cinema* will be published by the University of Texas Press. His works have been cited and reprinted extensively and have been translated into many languages, including French, German, Italian and Persian.

Gilane Tawadros is the founding Director of the Institute of International Visual Arts (inIVA) in London, an organisation which has been at the forefront of developments in contemporary visual art, new technologies and cultural diversity in both national and international contexts. Responsible for the overall artistic direction of inIVA, Tawadros has curated and co-curated a large number of exhibitions and edited several publications on contemporary visual art and theory. Previously, she has worked for the Photographers' Gallery and the Hayward Gallery, both in London, and has written and lectured internationally on contemporary visual arts.

Contributors' Biographies

Leila Ahmed
Christine Barthe
Bernina sewing machines
Lucy Collard
Charlotte Cotton
Sarah Graham-Brown
Salah Hassan
Aidan Higgins
Ally Ireson
Rose Issa
Michket Krifa
Rosemary Miles
John Picton

Acknowledgments